MW00909450

RIPPED

....

THE HAIRY TALES OF A
BRAZILIAN BIKINI WAXER

CHRISTINE DUQUETTE

Pacific Sky Press

Ripped: The Hairy Tales of a Brazilian Bikini Waxer. Copyright © 2011 by Christine Duquette. All rights reserved. No part of this publication may be reproduced, distributed or transmitted in any form or by any means, including photocopying, recording, or other electronic or mechanical methods, without the prior written permission of the publisher, except in the case of brief quotations embodied in critical reviews and certain other noncommercial uses permitted by copyright law. For permission requests, write to the publisher, addressed "Attention: Permissions Coordinator," at the address below.

Pacific Sky Press
PO Box 7545
Huntington Beach, CA 92615

This is a *mostly* true memoir. I have collected these stories from my own memories, memories in which I am likely smarter and funnier than others may remember. I have changed the names of some individuals and in some instances modified identifying features to preserve anonymity. In some cases, composite characters have been created and dialogue adjusted to maintain narrative flow.

Ripped: The Hairy Tales of a Brazilian Bikini Waxer/ Christine Duquette. -- 1st ed.

ISBN-13:978-0692602232

To my husband Gene, for letting me quit my job to write a book about vaginas and stuff.

If you want people to come over to your house honey, you have to clean things up a little.

—Bikini waxers everywhere

TABLE OF CONTENTS

....

BEHIND THE STICKY DOOR

Have you ever wanted to know what happens behind closed doors during a Brazilian bikini wax? I can tell you, and I *will*. For more than a decade, I have worked as an esthetician and Brazilian bikini waxer in Southern California, the very center of high-maintenance beauty.

Do you find yourself curious about what's under the hoods of the *real* Real Housewives of Orange County? I'll tell you. I'm an esthetician–a fancy, difficult-to-spell word for someone who gives facials and offers hair-removal waxing services professionally, as opposed to say, as a hobby. *That* person is called something else and there is probably a fetish group for them somewhere on the Internet.

Not every waxer is as comfortably acquainted with strangers' genitalia as I am; in fact, some estheticians won't even do a bikini waxing service for the very reason that it puts them in the near vicinity of flaps and sacs of all kinds. It is *precisely* all this flappy, fleshy nakedness that makes my job so interesting. Do you want to hear about your tax accountant's day or what it's like to work at a drycleaner? Or would you rather know what it's like to be up close and personal with this most intimate of services?

In a world of formalities and social masks, my job is a breath of fresh air, *mostly*. Have you ever been nervous and imagined everyone without his or her pants on in order to make you feel more comfortable? In my job, everyone *really* has their pants off. And yet, unlike a pelvic or prostate exam, there's no bad news, no paternal warnings to eat better, stop smoking or lay off the red meat.

I do many things in the course of my job, but Brazilian bikini waxing is what I do best. Perhaps it is the individual personality combination of my dominatrix side meshed with my mothering side, mixed with a side of attention-seeking only child, finished off with a sharp eye for detail that makes me just the right person to wax and tweeze your pubic hair into a perfectly coiffed garden or a smooth desert of skin.

So how did I end up a professional vagina waxer? There are many obvious reasons why I was attracted to this job: service trades, free beauty products, flexible hours, the chance to own my own business and of course, a job so removed from the rigid confines of corporate America that I was more free to be myself. The less obvious to me at the time, but very clear now, was that I absolutely yearned for female connection. Now before you make that something dirty and picture my staff and me in sexy lab coats pawing each other, know that this isn't that kind of book (except when it kind of is).

I think in hindsight I actually subconsciously picked my second career to have a built-in friend base. I had worked in a male-dominated company in a male-dominated industry for the bulk of my career and I was so over privately crying in the bathroom during my lunch hour and keeping any work drama in check. When you work in an industry filled with women, gay men and artists, you have much more freedom to express a full range of emotions, rollercoaster that they may be. I wanted more women and the energy they bring around me during my workday.

See, when you are in any one of the pink-collar beauty trades, there is almost zero male energy influencing how people behave. What few men there are often have an energy that is even more aggressively female than mine. Working with so many women sort of felt like boarding school for adults at times. Boil the job down to its essence, and working at a spa or salon can be a lot like a big girlie sleepover, but without the pillow fights, Ouija boards or lesbian experimentation.

Sure, like any job, my work as a Brazilian waxer has its downsides. I have done things I never thought I would do, like handle a stranger's testicles or try to think of a delicate way to tell someone she had some poop on her butt. I have been propositioned, cried on, invited into threesomes and robbed. I have waxed porn stars and old men on the same day and gone home with pubic hair stuck to my shoe more days than not. I have been shouted at, laughed with and pretty much everything in between. At the end of the day, I made some of the best friends I have ever had and while there were some bad days, they usually make for the best stories. So get undressed from the waist down and lay down right here on the table and I'll tell you a few doozies while we get you cleaned up.

ONE

....

MY FIRST TIME

Olga had arms the size of most women's thighs. She could have just as easily been a body builder or a butcher as an esthetician. A white lab coat covered a dress that belonged on an old-world Grandma and her coffee-colored, reinforced pantyhose poked through the toes of wicker-imprinted, white plastic sandals. She ushered me in to a space that looked more like an interrogation room than a day spa. A stark light dangled above a paper-covered table and a magnifying lamp in the corner dared you not to talk. On a rickety, rust-flecked metal stand was a pot filled with what I hoped was wax.

My flip-flops made suction noises as the soles tried to pull free of the flytrap floor, tacky with remnant wax. Olga commanded me to take off my clothes and get on the table. She stood there with her giant hands on her ample hips waiting for me. I looked around for either the changing area or a sign that she was going to leave the room so I could disrobe in private. No such luck. After an uncomfortable, fidgety moment, I realized Olga wasn't going anywhere and expected me to undress with her standing there waiting. I tried gracefully to remove my clothes but ended up clumsily tugging and pulling my jeans off, at one point hopping on one leg trying to free my foot. Then came the underwear, I had worn a cute pair thinking I should because I wouldn't be the only one seeing them. Now the choice of pink polka dots seemed ill-conceived and embarrassing. I put my clothes on a stool, stuffing my silly panties under my jeans.

This was my first introduction to bikini waxing, years before I would become a waxer myself. I don't remember when the impulse to be hair-free struck me, but I was a determined early adopter. No one I knew back then waxed more than their eyebrows and maybe their mustache. Sure a few women I knew were shaving a little off the top and sides of their bikini, but no one I knew was shucking off the whole works and they certainly were not letting a surly, three-hundred pound Russian woman do it. I opened my Yellow Pages and thumbed through the section on day spas. These were the early days of the Internet when it was used for porn and email, but not searching out local businesses and reviews. The majority of the day spas in my area were run by Eastern European women with names like Olga, Inga, Helga and Svetlana. They did facials, massage, waxing and quite possibly debt collection for the Russian mob.

It wasn't unusual to find waxing on spa menus but completely bare waxing was still the domain of porn stars and strippers. The average woman might get adventurous before a cruise and get a bikini wax, but that meant a quick rip of the hair that fell outside the traditional ribbed black maillot swimsuit of the every-woman. No one was asking anyone to wax their winkers or pluck their puckers. It took seven phone calls, a few snickers and one hang-up before I found a place willing to take it all off. Afraid I might lose my nerve if I had too long to think about it, I made my appointment for the following day.

So there I stood waiting for instructions from Olga. I tried to look nonchalant as my hands draped awkwardly over my naked bottom half.

"On your back," Olga motioned to the table with one of her turkey-leg arms.

Because of the height of the table, I had to climb on one leg at a time. This is *not* the preferred mounting position when you are pantiless.

I knew she would be seeing all of me during the procedure, but there is a reason why doctors leave the room to let you experience disrobing and gracelessly climbing atop the examination table all by yourself. I lay down, my vagina centered right under the hanging bulb. I smiled bravely at Olga, showing her I was a pro and this was no big deal. Her demeanor was like that of a pit bull and I thought that if I showed fear, it might make her more aggressive.

Ripped

Olga doused me in a cloud of baby powder and began to slather hot wax on my nether bits. The wax smelled like a mix of Christmas trees and Lysol and after the heat abated, it wasn't so bad, pleasant almost. I hunkered down on the table and let my body relax a bit. Then she pressed a piece of muslin, a fabric used to pull the wax off, over the wax she had covered me with and began to pull in rapid fire. I cried out in surprise.

"You no cry, it no hurt." she chastised me, not skipping a beat with her rips and pulls.

Oh but it did hurt. This is what I would think thirty minutes later when I was done. What I was thinking at that exact moment, as the white hot pain shot through my girl bits, was how to curb my fight or flight impulse to kick Olga hard in the jaw, shooting her straight into the other room giving me a safe distance to run, still bottomless, to my car. She ripped and ripped. She threw me into positions reminiscent of the former USSR's 11-year-old, double jointed gymnastics team—deftly and with one of her giant mitts until she had assaulted every possible nook in my cranny. Thirty excruciating minutes later, I was done. I fully expected to see blood and torn swaths of flesh hanging from the muslin strips but when I examined my goods, there was my lady business, pink, skin slightly puffy, but free of hair and almost illegally smooth. What happened next was what I now refer to as cha-cha cloud nine, Brazilian bliss, vagina Valhalla. This is when the pain of waxing triggers your brain to release endorphins that leave you feeling like you just took a handful of painkillers or ran for an hour. Screw runner's high, if you want to experience the same rush, just get a Brazilian wax. Admittedly, you may have to pray to Little Baby Jesus your vagina isn't being pulled from your body in order to get it.

I was happy and my vagina was the prettiest on the block or at least the YMCA changing room, which was the only place I typically saw other vaginas. Of course most of those other vaginas belonged to women collecting social security, so the bar was set pretty low. About three weeks later, I got my first crop of regrowth. Not every hair came back, probably only a third of them leaving me looking not unlike a bald guy with fresh hair plugs. I really wanted another Brazilian but I didn't have the courage to face Olga at the Gulag again. I went back to my Yellow Pages hoping to find a kinder, gentler version of my original tormentor. I settled on Sandy, a friendly, soft-spoken esthetician who seemed like the answer to my hairless prayers. I made my appointment, congratulating myself on my good fortune.

The day of my appointment, I arrived a few minutes early as Sandy settled up with her last client, a slow moving blue-hair carefully counting out sixty bucks in one-dollar bills. Sandy flashed me a nervous smile as I sat down in the small reception area. I sized her up as I waited. Something about her seemed somehow old-fashioned, like my friend Mare who had been raised by her grandparents. Sandy was tall and thin. She wore a red shirt with a straight black skirt and flats and her thin hair was tightly pulled back, making her look not unlike a dishwater-blonde Olive Oyl. After she finished checking out her client, she nervously introduced herself.

"Sandy is it okay if I use your restroom first?" I asked.

"Oh, sure, sure, it's right here," she said, pointing to a closed door.

"I'll just be a minute." I smiled, excusing myself.

I flipped on the light switch, pulled down my pants and perched on her toilet, looking around as I peed. A crystal bowl filled with dusty potpourri rested upon a white, distressed étagère in the corner of the bathroom. Several extra rolls of toilet paper were neatly hugged in a wicker cosy, and the soap dispenser was a pair of smiling cherubs. I finished up, gave myself a thorough wiping and washed my hands.

Stepping out of the restroom, Sandy showed me to a soft-lit room with a massage table draped in a pretty floral sheet. She had a small side table covered in velvet fabric with an immaculate wax pot filled to the brim and ready to go. This is more like it, I thought, giving myself an imaginary high-five.

"Okay, here you go," she said, motioning to a massage table, draped in soft sheets, "I'll be back in just a minute."

"Do you want me undressed," I asked, unsure. I didn't know if every waxer had the same procedure for this, and while this wasn't my first rodeo, it was only my second.

"Uh, you can leave your panties on I think, and you can put your things on that chair," she said as she pointed to a pretty chintz armchair in the corner.

Sandy shut the door behind her. I pulled my pants off and hoisted myself on the bed. I waited there for what seemed like ten minutes. Finally she knocked softly on the door and entered. She took a few deep breaths while looking anxiously around the room. She lit a candle and smiled or perhaps grimaced at me, it was hard to tell because of the dim mood-lighting. Sandy opened up a cellophane wrapped package of wooden tongue depressors and fished one out. She moved it from hand to hand a few times like she was trying to figure out how best to hold it. This was the first sign I had that perhaps Sandy was not an old hand at this. Actually it was the first sign I *noticed*. I should have caught on with the ambient lighting, the brand new, pristine wax pot and the good sheets on the bed. A seasoned waxer is far more likely to work with bright lights, disposable paper sheets and a wax pot that has seen its share of battles. My gut told me to get up, tell her I had changed my mind and calmly but quickly exit the establishment. The good and polite Midwesterner in me stayed glued to the table fingers crossed in hopes that this would go better than the signs were portending.

"Is this your place?" I asked, trying to make conversation.

"Yes. I opened it about a year ago." Sandy answered as she came over to me, her brows furrowed as she seemed to consider where to start.

"Where were you before?" I asked.

A few fine stray hairs peppered the edge of my thigh. Sandy buttered some wax on them, pressed a piece of muslin onto the wax and pulled. Voila, not bad at all. She stood admiring her handiwork as wax dripped from the spatula onto her flowery sheets.

"I did hair, nails and facials at Glenridge Oaks."

"I'm not familiar with that spa. Is it around here?" I asked.

Once she had removed the maybe twelve hairs that fell outside my undies she looked confused as to how she should proceed around my panties. She loaded the spatula with wax and carried it over to me, dripping as she went.

"It's not a spa, it's a retirement community."

She pushed the elastic leg of my undies over a bit and smoothed the wax on, but when she reached for a strip of muslin, she lost her grip and my undies snapped back to their usual position, firmly affixing themselves to the wax on my skin.

"Oops. I'm sorry. That wasn't supposed to happen," she apologized, chewing on the bottom of her lip.

She repeated the procedure on the other side with essentially the same result.

"Maybe it would be better if I take them off," I cautiously offered, again failing to recognize the glued-on panties as a sure sign to abort.

"That might be better," she agreed.

I rolled off of the bed, hitting several globs of wax on my way off. I moved away from the bed to put my undies with the rest of my clothes and the sheet, stuck to my body in several places, dragged with me. Sandy stepped in and pulled the sheet from my legs where it was stuck. She looked like she might actually cry. I tried to remove my underwear, but realized I'd have to start from one side. It felt like I had been duct-taped in some kind of complicated sorority hazing ritual. I reasoned that faster was better, like pulling a Band-Aid off. I peeled them off and gave myself two bright raspberries where I tugged the skin too hard.

Sandy had spread the sheet back on the bed. I hobbled up–the walking wounded, shoring up for the next assault, like GIs barely healed sent back into battle. Sandy slipped into what I can only assume was her panic mode. She paced and teetered from one end of the room to another like one of those round robot vacuum cleaners that hits a wall and changes direction. She finally came to rest by the side of the bed, seemingly determined to finish the job. She had me move my leg to the side, like a flamingo, and tried to wax my inner thigh. After several painful tugs, the wax strip came off, leaving most of the wax behind. She just kept going, ready to go down with this ship if necessary. A few drips and rips later, she tried to clean me up but left me feeling like a scrubbed, peeled, and sticky potato.

She put all of her stuff down and looked at me.

"All done!" she chirped insanely and left the room.

Getting up was a feat, considering the random bits of lip stuck to thigh and my butt cheeks nearly welded together. I tried to pull on my panties but they were a lost cause. Stuck together like a wad of gum, I abandoned them in Sandy's pretty floral trash can. I pulled on my clothes and every step I took, some piece of my skin pulled away from another. I bravely edged to the counter and Sandy gave me a little handwritten ticket with my bill on it.

"I had to charge you a little extra because it took so long," she said.

Wanting only to be out of that place before Stockholm syndrome took hold, I smiled weakly and thrust my credit card at her. I think I may have even left her a tip. Once home, I inspected the damage under my real bathroom lighting, as opposed to the spa's boudoir lighting. I had two oozing stripes where my lips used to be and various purple bruises that made it look like I was attacked by a roving band of hickey fetishists. I had wax all over me and my skin looked like a lobster had mated with a plucked chicken. Two containers of baby oil, several showers, and liberal applications of antibiotic wound cream later, I was physically healing, but the nightmare of the experience was still fresh in my mind. I was certain that if Sandy, a trained esthetician could fumble so horribly, then the fact that someone was licensed was little or no promise that they could actually do the job. I decided that, like sex with my college boyfriend, if I wanted something done right, I was going to have to do it myself.

A few weeks later, a trip to my local beauty supply left me seventy-five dollars lighter and ready to do some DIY on my very own front yard. I come from a long line of women who permed their own hair and bleached their own mustaches– this was in my *blood*. There was no way I was going to pay for the privilege of near public pubic humiliation when I could wax my cha from the safety and privacy of my own home. I got my loot home and approached the job with pioneer spirit. I had a beach date the following day with Salvador, an artist I had been seeing, and I was determined to be silky smooth in my swimsuit.

I carefully laid out my tools and skimmed the scant, confusing directions included with the wax. I stripped down and perched on the seat of my bathroom toilet. I was at a precipice, a jumping off point that in the years to come would turn into a career, a business, and later this book. But I didn't know any of this then, I was just a girl with some professional beauty products and bad directions translated from Chinese. This is going to be like doing nose pore strips and peel off facial masks, *totally* fun, I convinced myself. Unlike Olga, I started with very small areas, careful to judge my pain threshold and technique before moving forward. There was some breath-holding, some yoga moves, some cursing and more than a little crying, but an hour and a half later, I was all done. I looked my goodies over and I had done a surprisingly good job. Still a little sticky, I cleaned myself off but it was getting late and I figured the rest would come off in the shower the following day. My bathroom was the real victim. It took me longer to clean up my mess than it had to wax. Tendrils of wax hung from my toilet seat and drippy globs of wax pooled on the floor. Still, mission accomplished. I went to bed worn out, self-satisfied and looking forward to the next day's date, a theater to show off my handiwork.

The next day, I showered and readied myself for lunch and a day at the beach. I still felt a little residue left from the waxing but you couldn't even see it. My thighs and cooter looked smooth and the redness that was there the night before was now gone. This was only my third date with Salvador so I wanted to make a good impression. I had new jeans, a new top, a new swimsuit and a fifty-dollar pedicure–I was ready. The jeans were a dark wash and I pulled them out of the bag, ripped the tags off with my teeth and jumped and shimmied myself into them. I assembled the rest of my outfit and admired myself in the mirror. I looked good. Grabbing my keys, I headed out the door.

When Salvador greeted me in front of the café, he looked me over, nodded appreciatively and gave my bum a little pat. We talked and flirted through lunch, taking breaks just long enough to eat some of our food. I listened dutifully as Salvador filled me in on the intricacies of his newest gallery show. The theme of the show was hands, just hands he told me emphatically as he put his hands a little too close to my face to make the point. There are hands working, hands soothing, hands fighting, he told me. While he talked, I imagined myself his next muse, a series of photographs devoted only to my bum. My bum resting on a velvet bench, my bum swathed in transparent gauze, my bum encased in bubble wrap; there were all kinds of possibilities. It registered momentarily that he really liked to talk about himself, but he was a beautiful man who might immortalize my posterior for posterity and so I endured. Salvador paid for lunch, pulled out my chair and put his hand on the small of my back as we walked out of the restaurant. We got our swim stuff and hit the beach-side bathrooms. Heading into the women's, there was a stall with two metal walls but no door. I took off my clothes and shoved them into my beach bag. I pulled on the new swimsuit and though there were no mirrors, I just *knew* I looked good. I did one double check to make sure I had removed all the price tags when I saw my thighs and gasped in horror. The once invisible wax residue running the length of my inner thigh was now the color of an angry, violet bruise. I looked at the identical injuries on my thighs confused until I realized that dyed fibers from my new pants had clung to the leftover wax, making it look like I had either been riding an incredibly violent horse or someone had spent hours riding *me*. I panicked and grabbed fistfuls of the rough paper towels, wet them and tried furiously to rub the fuzz-coated wax off. The wax stuck, so I pressed a nearby soap dispenser until my wad of paper towels was covered with the iridescent pink of cheap bathroom soap. This has got to work, I prayed as I scrubbed in all directions. The fuzz was better, faded now to the light blue of an older bruise but now angry red streaks covered my thighs. After ten minutes of scrubbing, I left the bathroom defeated hoping it wasn't noticeable. I tried not to draw attention to it but I was tarred and feathered. Salvador never mentioned my battered bottom half but that was the last date we had. I imagine that he did a series of photographs of disembodied torsos, bruised and sticky, rather than the tribute to my rear I hoped for. Leaving wax behind was a rookie mistake, but I was a rookie. I had done okay, but I vowed to get better.

....

TWO

WHAT THEY DON'T TEACH YOU IN BEAUTY SCHOOL

I wanted to follow up the story of the first Brazilian I *received* with the story of the first Brazilian I *gave* but honestly, I can't remember that first. Those first Brazilians are sort of a blur, probably due to PTSD. When I first started offering Brazilian waxing to my clients, I was awful. Not butt-weldingly torn flesh awful, but pretty bad. My first waxes took longer, hurt more and left my clients more beat up than later when I had honed my skills.

A Brazilian wax is among the most challenging services an esthetician will perform. It requires a level of skill and precision that other waxing services don't. It's kind of like the difference between a doctor listening to someone's lungs and looking into their ears versus performing a pelvic exam or colonoscopy. First, it's personal, there is touching and nudity involved. Second, it's different than a leg wax or upper lip wax. The parts are squishy and flappy and delicate and easy to injure so you have to place and remove wax more carefully. There is a definite technique required to perform a Brazilian wax well, and like most things, the more practiced you are the better you do.

Ripped

When I was getting licensed, most beauty schools didn't really teach you the ins and outs of Brazilian waxing. In fact, they didn't really teach you to be a good esthetician at all, only a *safe* esthetician. Even the beauty school exams and state licensing were mostly designed to see if you knew when you should wash your hands, how to disinfect your implements or why you shouldn't use something on a client after you've dropped it on the floor. It was very much the same with cosmetologists. Our respective states license us to protect you the patron from health risks but not from a terrible Brazilian wax or a bad dye job. Think about *that* the next time you go in for a beauty service. It's a big, beautiful game of Russian roulette so ask around for referrals before you get in someone's chair or on their table.

So why was something as difficult as a Brazilian wax service left off the beauty school curriculum? First, Brazilian waxing was just starting to be a thing here in the states. All of the instructors at the school I attended were in their sixties and their course instruction was at least a decade, if not more, behind the industry trends. I don't think my instructors understood that this area of waxing offered a huge potential money maker for graduating estheticians. Second, Brazilian waxing is an intimate service and is not something everyone *wants* to learn. Not surprisingly, being elbow deep in muffs, butts and pubes are not everyone's idea of the world's greatest job. Third, in beauty school, our 'spa room' was just one communal classroom with about eight massage tables so that our instructors could observe and guide our treatments. There wasn't really the privacy needed to do cha-cha waxing. And last, our victims, I mean clients, were typically elderly women who were drawn to the ultra-cheap services the beauty school offered. These were not the women who were clamoring for vagina waxing, they wanted facials and their chin whiskers waxed.

Even practicing among ourselves, which we did with all of the other services, was limited. If you wanted someone to let you wax their cha-cha for practice, you had to be willing to let them wax yours–quid pro quo. I found only one woman in class brave enough to swap services with but she graduated and moved on before I could get any better. So when I graduated, received my license from the state of California and opened my own spa, I was already very good and practiced at most services, but the Brazilian bikini wax was not among them.

How do you learn something that they didn't teach you in beauty school but that clients are willing to pay good money for? You practice on anyone that will let you. So when a few of my first clients asked for more than a basic bikini wax, I had to use them for practice knowing they would likely never come back. While it didn't feel right to say yes to something I didn't really know how to do, it was the only way I would get the practice I needed to learn what worked. I am fairly certain that in those early days of operating my spa, I ruined waxing for at least a handful of women. And as hard as it was on them, it was hard on me too. I had to feign comfort while I got used to seeing people so naked, so close up. I had to pretend to be confident and banter while at the same time intensely focusing on the task before me. I had to put aside my fear of touching naked strangers and get used to picking waxy pubic hair off of my fingernails. I also had to keep getting Brazilian waxes from a bevy of professionals as I tried to learn, refine my technique and get better by observing how others did it.

So, these first waxes I don't remember in any detail. I do remember being really nervous and I can recall the anxious feeling that settled in every time I saw a Brazilian wax service scheduled on my calendar. And I remember a fellow esthetician telling me to just pretend I knew what I was doing and the clients wouldn't know the difference. But I think my mind has blocked most of it out, not wanting to recall the cringe-worthy beginnings of my Brazilian waxing days. In my mind now I don't even see a flurry of faces just a hazy mental slideshow of anxiety-inducing cha-chas if anything. But I can remember *one* first, and that was the first male Brazilian bikini wax I did. That was unforgettable.

THREE

....

MANSCAPING THE MANZILIAN

never thought about waxing testicles in beauty school. Not surprisingly, it never really came up. Neither of my late middle-aged, platinum blonde, heavily made-up beauty-school teachers ever looked me straight in the eyes and said Chris, if you really want to make some serious cash in this business, you are going to have to get very comfortable holding a man's junk while you slather hot wax on it. Had I known that male waxing was to become a good chunk of my regular business, I would have probably gone to law school like I originally planned to. Anything that involves guys, genitalia, and payment seems understandably suspect. I never planned to include male waxing as part of my service menu. If some random guy had called the spa looking for a Brazilian wax, I would have said no faster than a stripper's affections change when you've maxed out your Visa.

The first *manzilian* I *manscaped* was James, the boyfriend of Tess, a longtime client of mine. This eased me into a service that I would eventually become very familiar with. I was confident James wasn't a creep or looking for some kind of happy ending. Tess told me he'd been shaving downstairs and she was getting good and tired of a razor-burned cha-cha from his *stuff scruff*. I leveled with her: I had never performed a bikini wax on a male client before, but if he were willing and at least a little brave, I would do my very best. I knew the procedure was going to take me longer than usual because I'd have to work slowly and carefully; it's not just the top triangle that gets waxed, it's the squishy bits too. James was game–at least Tess told me he was–and she said she'd be there in case I needed an extra set of hands.

On the day of the appointment, I got everything ready and tried to steel myself against the jitters. Why would I voluntarily do this, you may wonder? There is a large gay community around the spa and male pubic-grooming among both straight and gay men was becoming very popular. I knew that if I could get comfortable with this service that very few estheticians are willing to perform, I could charge more than a female wax and I would have another revenue stream coming into the spa. I could have a virtual man-meat monopoly. If I charge seventy-five dollars for a manzilian and it takes me twenty minutes on average, then I'm grossing an average of two-hundred-twenty-five dollars an hour, not to mention tips. Comparable perhaps to what my hourly might have been had I gone to law school as planned, with much more interesting stories to tell at cocktail parties.

So they arrived and, to my surprise, Tess's boyfriend was a colossal, rock solid, towering African-American man. He was a personal trainer, a competition weight lifter and ripped with muscle. He looked like Leonardo's David if David had added a few more arm and leg days each week at the gym. I am just over five feet tall so with his height and bulk, James was physically intimidating. Admittedly, I had never seen a black man naked, up close and personal. It's not that race made a difference, but for the first manzilian I ever did, I guess I was secretly hoping for a small, spongy white boy that would lie prostrate to my dominatrix-like maneuvering.

James, Tess, and I proceeded to the treatment room. I directed him to the changing room door where I told him that I would need him naked from the waist down. I had put a hand towel in there—what I now refer to as the 'dignity towel,' so that he could cover himself. To my surprise, he swaggered out completely naked, sans towel of any kind.

"There's a towel in there you can use to cover up a bit," I offered, trying not to look directly at his equipment.

"I don't need a towel," he said and shrugged. He was obviously very proud of his form, with good reason.

"Well, the towel is for me too. You do want me focused on the area I'm applying hot wax to, yes?" I gently admonished him.

He looked me straight in the eye and volleyed one right at me, "Then I'm going to need a bigger towel."

"That towel will do just fine," I hit back.

James held the towel against his groin, sat down on the table and swung his legs over as he lay down. The padded massage table was way too small for all six feet six inches of him. His lower legs stuck awkwardly off the edge of the table and he had to keep his arms crossed over his chest to keep them from dangling over the sides. It was like laying a Ken doll on a deck of cards.

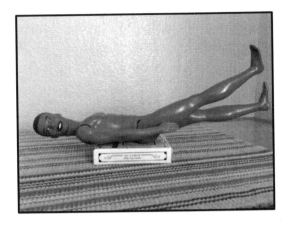

I found this doll online and knew it would be perfect for showing how tall James looked on my small table. I kept the doll in my nightstand waiting to set up the picture. One day I was cleaning out my drawer and my *middlest* daughter, ten at the time, came in and was chatting with me. When I pulled out James doll and set him on the bed to wipe out the bottom of the drawer, she said, "Mom, why do you have a black Barbie doll in your bedside drawer? Wait, never mind, I don't think I want to know."

I had James keep his legs straight and the dignity towel over his bits and bobs. I placed his hand on top of the towel to keep his junk taut and powdered the top triangle area.

He wasn't aroused, though now I know it does happen, but the soft dusting of powder seemed to put him at ease. Then I slathered on some of the warm wax and taking a deep breath, he relaxed even more.

"Mmm, warm." he noted and looked up at me benevolently.

His girlfriend looked smugly expectant, like she knew something he didn't, something she couldn't wait for him to find out.

I smoothed the fabric over the wax, careful not to do any unnecessarily vigorous rubbing and he sank into the table as if to say, this isn't so bad. Then I grasped the strip firmly and pulled.

I have never seen a black man go *pale* before, but I am absolutely certain he changed shades. He grimaced and let out a little yelp. His girlfriend laughed, "Now you see what I go through for you? And you thought it was going to be *easy*, fool."

His manhood in question, he braced himself for the next pull. To his credit, he didn't make a sound but his autonomic nervous system took over for him and he began sweating profusely.

Now to get a good wax, you have to keep the area you are waxing dry, hence the powder. Because James was sweating so much, I had to mop up his sweat with a stack of paper towels in between waxing, otherwise everything would end up a sticky, gooey mess. More waxing and mopping, I was working so hard at that point that now *I* was sweating and between the two of us, the room had to be ninety degrees. A few more pat downs with the paper towel, slathers, and rips and I was done with the top. I prepared to move south.

Waxing the area of his pubic bone, the triangle if you will, was no big deal because, besides the fact that there is less fatty tissue and it's hairier, it almost the same as it is on a woman. Now for the jumping-off point. Yes, I was about to wax his guys.

Now lest you come to the same conclusion as my mother-in-law that I am some sort of trollopy sex worker, know this, I am *very* comfortable with nudity. I am also very comfortable with people in general, especially when they are vulnerable because they are naked and I have my clothes on. I think it appeals to my introverted nature. You know how your mom used to tell you when you were nervous about giving a speech that you should just imagine everyone naked in their socks and you wouldn't feel so intimidated? Well, that's how waxing is: you are sitting there naked on my table while I'm in the position of trying to make *you* feel comfortable.

So I smoothed some oil over his skin and yes, by skin I mean scrotum skin, and although I appear calm on the outside, I am so embarrassed. I'd never been in a situation where a penis in front of me wasn't my plaything. I wasn't attracted to him or wishing the lights were dim and we were all alone but the very fact that it wasn't sexual at all made it weird to be in the same room as a naked man, oh, and his girlfriend. At that point, I was trying to be very professional and matter-of-fact, like, *oh yeah, I do this all the time, nothing making me feel awkward here folks*, but I was *beyond* uncomfortable.

Plus on top of the awkwardness of the intimacy of this service with a near stranger, I was now about to perform a service I never had before and that would be enough to make anyone nervous. The first time you do anything is hard, even harder when there's nudity and pain involved. I was having visions in my head of pulling the wrong way and something tearing off and flying across the room.

So everything was oiled and I had positioned his hand over the dignity towel covering his penis. I had him hold everything taut toward him and began the sac wax. The key here, I have learned, is to work in very small strips.

I smoothed some wax on, let it cool and *riiiip*.

Repeat.

James was doing pretty good at this point because those natural pain endorphins had kicked in. His eyes were just sort of glazed over and he looked a bit shell-shocked. Testicles are, without a doubt, the hardest things to wax. They are the hardest precisely because they are the *softest* and they are remarkably pliable. Getting them to stay in one place while you wax them is challenging. I stretched and twisted them (I can't believe his balls are getting their own pronoun) like bread dough, pressed and ripped until they were smooth. It took me a while but he was nearly hair free–nearly.

One of the things that make a Brazilian a Brazilian is the ass wax. Yes, if you haven't had the bum done, you've been shortchanged.

"James, I'm going to need you to pull your knees into your chest," I said, "like this," pulling my own bent leg toward my chest to demonstrate. I never wax people on their hands and knees like many other estheticians do, it's too degrading and not the best position anyway.

"You want me to *what?*" he asked, clearly very confused as to what was coming next.

"I'm going to wax your winker and that will *complete* the Brazilian service," I told him. James looked pleadingly at his girlfriend and she returned it with a steely gaze, "Oh just do it, you've come this far."

The good thing about the ass wax is that although it can be humiliating for some people because, you know, that's where your poop comes from, it hardly hurts at all. So reluctantly he got into position and three easy rip-rip-rips later, I was done. I removed the remaining wax residue, and smoothed on some icy aloe gel to cool down his skin.

"You're done. Go ahead and get dressed and I'll meet you up front."

Ripped

I went up to the front desk and collapsed in my chair, but not before grabbing a freezing cold Diet Coke from the little fridge. All of my adrenaline circuits had been pumping full blast so now I was exhausted. Thank god I had my lab coat on because my shirt underneath was soaked. I had perspired so much that I was positively dehydrated.

I sat in my chair drinking my soda and waiting for them, and by them I mean James and Tess, not James' testicles. There's one more thing I love about the Brazilian. Though quite unnecessarily, many people must feel a bit bad that you've had to be in such close contact with their naughty parts–moving aside lips and balls, face to face with parts even their loved ones have never seen so close, and in such bright light–so they tip great.

James and his girlfriend came up front. He was no longer swaggering but looked more like a guy who had just had outpatient kidney surgery. He thrust a thick wad of bills out toward me like it was hush money and I never saw him again.

....

FOUR

MY MOTHER-IN-LAW THINKS I'M A WHORE

We were snuggling in bed in a haze of post-coital bliss when my then boyfriend, now husband dropped a bomb on me.

"I told my mom we're planning on getting married," he said, somehow making it feel more real by saying the words out loud.

"You did?"

"Yeah, I did," he said, squeezing his arms around me tighter, burying his face in my neck.

I put my hands up to his chest and pushed him away from me so I could see his face. "What did she say?" I probed, curious about my future mother-in-law's opinion of our decision to take this giant leap together.

"Well, she said she was happy for me," he paused trying to go back in for the snuggle, "and of course, she said she had some concerns."

"Concerns?" I asked flatly, as a small surge of adrenaline coursed through my body, alerting all of my nerves.

"You know my mom," he said offhandedly, "no big deal, in fact it was pretty funny, you would have gotten a kick out of it." He smiled and shook his head.

"I would have, huh? So what *exactly* did she say?"

"Do you really want to know?"

"Yes, I *really* do."

This should have been his sign to abort. He should have immediately redirected this line of conversation or offered to run out for Thai food, give me a back rub or buy me shoes. Barring that, he should have made up something benign like she was concerned about a wedding in fall that it might rain, or concerned that he wasn't going to buy a ring big enough to suit someone like me, or concerned that she'd have enough time to plan a proper shower, anything, *anything* but the truth. But one thing about my husband that I love when I am questioning him and hate when he is trying to negotiate anything is that he is a terrible liar, so terrible that he almost never attempts it.

"Well, she said," he chuckled a little while my eyes drilled into his, waiting for it–just what was it that she was, ahem, concerned about anyway. "She said she had some concerns that your, uh, your, you know, your business is not entirely above board."

"*Excuse* me?"

"I think her exact words were that there might be some 'funny business going on in the back'," he smiled and shook his head, remembering the conversation.

I couldn't control it, I pushed him away from me, my eyes welled up, my chest tightened and I started to cry.

"Oh, my god, I shouldn't have told you, should I?" His face crumpled into concern and he pulled me toward him.

29

"Probably not," I sputtered.

"I just thought it was funny–you know my mom, totally paranoid and overblowing everything, it's not a big deal."

"Your mom thinks I'm a *whore*," I said through the wet mess that had become my face.

"No she doesn't think you're a whore, she *likes* you," he tried to reassure me.

"She insinuated that I am giving *hand jobs* in the back room. Or *worse*."

"Well, kind of, yeah, she kind of did. You know she likes you though, right?"

I wasn't even listening to him anymore, spiraling into my own anger and disbelief. "Do you know how hard I worked to open the spa? Do you know home much sweat equity I put into it, how much dry walling I did, how many nights I spent eating ramen so I could conserve money until the business got busier, how much schlepping I did to get people in the front door? For her to even hint that I am successful for anything other than my own hard work is incredibly insulting and hurtful."

"I am so sorry," he said, "I thought you would think it was funny like I did."

"I probably will someday," I said sniffling, "right now it's just making me sad." I started to cry all over again.

"I really…" he paused, "Chris…if I thought it was going to upset you, I wouldn't have told you. I thought we were going to have a good laugh over my mom." He hugged me tighter, "*I* know how smart you are and how hard you worked to start your business."

Later that day I found myself getting more upset every time I thought about it. How dare she minimize my accomplishments by suggesting I was basically little more than a prostitute. How dare she undermine a female victory through the verbal equivalent of smashing my kneecaps. I got out my phone and called the one person I knew would understand and of course, take my side–my mother.

I told her everything that happened, just waiting for her rage to boil over at the very thought of someone suggesting her daughter was a trollop. I knew my mother, a female business person herself, would understand the insult to my human dignity, the affront to my education and the minimization of my accomplishments. I rattled off the whole story, getting more worked up as I told her, ready for the inevitable lashing she was going to give my future mother-in-law.

It took my mom a good five minutes to stop laughing.

"Oh Christy, that is just about the funniest thing I think I've ever heard."

"It is not funny, she basically called me a *hooker.*"

"Well, not really, it's just that generation, you know?" There is nearly a twenty-year age gap between my mother and my mother-in-law.

"Remember how Grandma and Grandpa wouldn't get a massage with us until we practically dragged them? Grandma still asks if it's 'one of them funny places or not' when I take her for a massage. It's that whole generation–they don't understand paying someone to do any kind of personal grooming beyond a crew cut and a perm."

"This was not the outrage I was looking for. Where is your solidarity?"

"Oh, it's really pretty funny if you get over yourself."

MY MOTHER-IN-LAW THINKS I'M A WHORE

How did I make the leap from esthetician to prostitute in my mother-in-law's eyes? My husband had made the mistake of telling her that I did Brazilian bikini waxing. He likewise failed to leave out a detail I certainly would have–that I also do *male* bikini waxing. My mother-in-law is in her seventies and completely removed from the generation of women and men who do any sort of pubic grooming, much less use hot wax to take it all off. Yes, my mother-in-law thought I might be making my living giving reach-arounds or worse but with the nature of a Brazilian wax, it wasn't *that* far a leap. Of course she didn't seem at all hesitant about visiting a *cathouse* when the free massages and facials were flowing. The first time she visited the spa, I had to rein in my urge to post a sign in back that read, "Hand jobs, thirty bucks extra. Want something special? Just ask!" I'm sure that would have gone over well. Even after having published this book, she will probably still think I'm a whore, albeit a reformed one. Why else would people buy a book about waxing unless it was a tell-all exposé about all of those hand jobs I was doling out in the back? I want to finally admit for the record that yes, I was giving a bunch of hand jobs in the back room. And you know what? I wasn't even charging, I was just doing it for fun.

Family is funny. You know they have been quick to point out I am a professional pimple popper and pube peruser but they are also the first ones in line for free stuff. When I was first in beauty school, I welcomed the opportunity to ply my trade and practice on willing family. Freebies were given like Christmas bonuses; a bikini wax for my cousin, an eyebrow shaping for my aunt, an eyelash tinting for my grandma, a facial for my mom, no problem. Of course, ten years later and they still tell me I can practice on them. Lucky me right? After years of having my own space, with all of my equipment at hand, a comfortable chair and a sink, there is nothing I like more than rubbing someone's face with whatever was in their medicine cabinet while they lay prone across their bed. And yes, I have waxed the cha of friends and relatives alike on a towel spread on my living room floor while watching Law & Order– that really happened. Family will still occasionally offer up theirs, like waxing yet another vag, for free mind you, is some kind of reward, you can do mine if you want, oh really can I? Uh, maybe next time.

As willing as I am to lend my able hands to waxing the bush of my brethren, there is one punani I do not want to peer into–that of my mother. First, I don't want to see the vagina I came out of. I already have plenty of material to keep my therapist busy for a lifetime. Second, my mother and I have the same hands. When I look at her hands, I get a preview of what mine will look like in twenty years. I don't really want to see a family resemblance or an aging vag timeline. Not that I would be able to see anything any-how, given that she sports the equivalent of mom jeans on her bush, it's all about Bob Ross fro-style full coverage.

In the middle of beauty school, I went home to visit for a long holiday weekend. We students had practiced waxing so much that we all had the thinnest eyebrows, no bush, even our arms were hairless. We'd all drool over the hairy new crop of students each month.

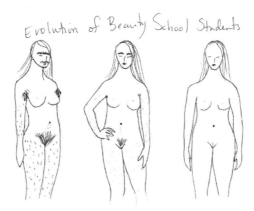

Okay so maybe this is a bit of an exaggeration. Most of us never started out that hairy but by the time we graduated, most of us didn't have
eyebrows.

I arrived home hairless and ready to enjoy the weekend on the
lake with friends and family. I was changing into my swimsuit
when my mother walked in without knocking, of course. Boundaries have never been her strong suit. She looked right at my hairless cha.

"What, huh, what did you, where did it...?" she stammered.

"Mom," I said, shielding myself, "get out."

"Where's your hair, what did you do?"

"I waxed it off, can you get out of here please?"

"Sandy you have to come see this," she shouted down the hall
to her high-school friend who was visiting.

Now in all fairness, Sandy is like a mother to me and I have
known her all of my life, but I did not want any more witnesses to
the family freak show. I pushed my mom out and shut the door,
feeling like I was twelve instead of twenty. All day long I had to
hear about it. "Like a plucked chicken," "you can see *everything*,"
"smooth as a slice of bologna." I even had to hear my grandma tell

me that as she aged most of her hair stopped growing "down there" so ours probably looked the same. Uh, no they don't, Grandma, and saying otherwise is not okay.

Beyond the crazy of my extended family, waxing has had an unintended impact on my children. We are not the naked McNakedersons, but I am also not the most modest person. My girls see me naked all the time and they are unfazed because all three of us look the same–hairless. Peru isn't the only place experiencing mass deforestation. Since I hit my twenties, I have always sported a bare muff. I never thought much about the fact that my girls had not seen a woman with pubic hair until my older daughter came home from a weekend of swimming at Grandmas and told me with her face all scrunched up that "grandma has spiders there," pointing at her crotch. This made me realize that because my husband is the only one in our family of five that sports any bush, my son has probably come to associate pubes with masculinity.

"You need to have a talk with the boy about pubic hair," I told my husband.

"Sure," he answered absentmindedly. A few minutes later, he stuck his head in the office.

"Why exactly do I need to talk to him about pubic hair?"

"Because someday he is going to get to third base."

"And?" he asked confused, "I thought we already talked to him about this."

"Well, if you remember correctly, *I* talked to him, after buying him a very nice book, because apparently, I am the driver of the puberty train. Anyhow, someday, he is going to get to third base and get freaked out when he discovers girls have pubic hair too."

"Third base? How many times have I told you, I don't understand your sports metaphors? Anyhow, is this *really* a problem that requires a conversation?"

"Honey, he has seen me and the girls nekkid and none of us have any cha-cha hair. By the time the girls are sprouting their first ones, they will *not* be walking around nudey pants in front of their older brother anymore. He will grow up thinking women are naturally hairless. What if he dates a hippie or something, he might get grossed out and scar them both."

"We've already had the talk with him about the whole puberty thing. I think he understands that women have pubic hair. The book you got him went into hair didn't it? If not, I will just pick up the next installment of the Harry Potter series."

"Huh?"

"You know, Harry Potter and the Pernicious Pubes and Perilous Pimples." He said, smiling at his own cleverness.

"Can you please just have a conversation with him about pubic hair?"

"But you are so much better at these conversations than I am."

"That's because I have the most practice and anyhow, if I'm always the one who has the talks with him, he's going to get the idea that I am obsessed with pubic hair or something."

"Chris, it's your job and you are writing a book about it, I think that ship has sailed."

....

NOTHING SCREAMS CLASSY LIKE A HOT PINK COOTER

I love strippers, and for totally different reasons than my dad does. Because of the necessary vagina maintenance inherent in their job, I have worked on *mounds* of strippers. I love strippers because they say more inappropriate things than I do and that is not an easy feat. Strippers also know how to tip. As a rule, strippers tip much better than, for instance, teachers. That's something to think about. But teachers teach our kids, so yeah, that's good too. There is also the camaraderie inherent in the fact that we both spend a great deal of time around vaginas. I mean the strippers, not the *teachers*, unless maybe they are gym teachers at an all-girls school. The other good thing about my exotic dancing clientele is that they have pushed me professionally. Strippers do things that most of us only think about, or more likely would *never* think about, like vajazzle their lady business with superglue and rhinestones and wear sexy nurse costumes on a day other than Halloween. Every time I think I have become entirely accustomed to this unconventional group of women, I am surprised anew.

"I have a special request," Natalie told me over the phone. Natalie was an exotic dancer and a surprisingly shrewd businesswoman. She was always looking for ways to up her game and rake in more bills than her fellow dancers.

"Lay it on me," I said.

"I want to do something special for Valentine's Day. I was thinking about a heart."

I hadn't done a heart before but I figured it's just a triangle with the top turned inward a bit, easy enough.

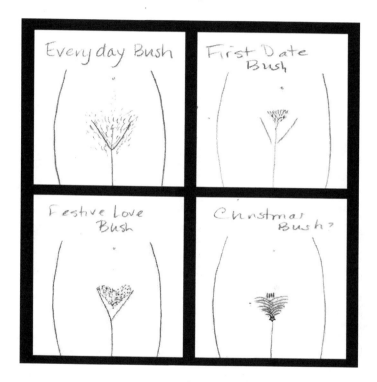

"Sure, as long as you have enough hair to define the shape, I can do a heart."

"I have another request."

"Of course you do."

"I want it pink, you know, the hair, the heart, it should be pink."

"Are you coming in with it pink already or do you need me to dye it for you?"

"I was hoping you could do it, I've never colored my pussy before."

"This would be a first for me too." I paused, the gears moving in my head. "We could probably use pink hair tint, something like Manic Panic but you'd need to bleach out the hair first for it to actually take." I was thankful I had paid attention to the cosmetology girls while they sucked on Salems on our lunch breaks back in the heady days of beauty school.

"What am I gonna do about the roots?"

I thought back to the ill-fated Burgundy temporary tint I put in my light blonde hair in homage to Madonna's *Like a Prayer* days that left me with pink-tinged hair for an entire college semester. "Wax it all off and start over?" I offered.

Natalie scheduled an appointment for a few days later and I set about procuring the necessary items to get the job done.

The day of her appointment Natalie breezed in, all legs, hair extensions and deliberate sexuality. She followed me into the waxing room and slipped out of her jeans before I could even open my mouth.

"I can't tell you how badly I have needed you, look at *this*," she implored, pointing aggressively to her modest bikini regrowth. "Am I a Sasquatch or what? Or better yet, a Sa-snatch," she said, making herself laugh.

"Oh, that's not so bad," I offered.

"Well, unexpectedly, I made a few new fans because of my giant bush. I don't know, maybe they are nature lovers. This French guy spent the whole night with me, practically maxed out his Visa. *"Why no the girls have zee booush,"* she mimicked. "I guess no one has pubes anymore. Still, I am glad to whack it back, I am starting to feel a bit furry."

"It's interesting," I offered, "to know that there is a market for hair. Perhaps if you tire of waxing, you can bill yourself as Nanette, the French all-natural au pair?"

"Oooo la la," she growled.

"Okay," I said, getting down to business, "we need to bleach it first." I pulled out the cream bleach I had seen in the medicine cabinets of nearly all of the women in my family. I inherited my father's fair skin and blonde hair so I grew up absent the knowledge of how to bleach facial hair that was passed along to the brunettes in the family. Because of this, I was left a bit flummoxed about the bleaching itself. Hmm, I thought, sizing up Natalie's crotch, couldn't be much different than my mother's moustache right? Just a little lower.

I mixed the bleach according to the directions and gently frosted it on her pubes. "I think I am going to have to comb this through, so that it gets on all of the hair."

"You are going to comb my pubic hair?" She snorted, her legs bending up in reflexive embarrassment.

"Stop," I said, pushing her legs back down, "you're going to get the bleach all over. It's not like I'm braiding it," I retorted. "Anyway, you have men shove dollar bills in your butt crack, what are you embarrassed about?"

"It's weird, that's all."

"Weirder than a hot pink pussy?"

"You're probably right," she said as she tried to compose herself. She straightened her legs, took a deep breath and tried to relax.

While she sat with the bleach on, she filled me in on the rest of her week. I wiped a little off checking every few minutes as the hair morphed from brown to light brown to orange to yellow then finally to a pale yellow.

"Done," I said, wiping the gritty paste off her.

"Holy shit, I look like Billy Idol," she said, admiring her platinum puss.

"Ready for the pink?"

"*That's* what *he* said!" she joked.

I left off my gloves figuring I could work more neatly and better control where the pink dye went without them. I used a spatula and mask brush and tried to delicately apply the pink without getting it all over Natalie's skin. I felt like a toddler finger painting as I furiously wiped bits and blobs of tint off of her. As her hair began to process, I went to wash my hands realizing that my fingers were haplessly stained fuchsia. I knew the job was dangerous when I took it. The tint worked much faster than the bleach and in a matter of minutes Natalie looked like she had a hot pink boa shoved between her legs.

"Okay, now for the fun part," I said, as I prepared her for the final wax step.

"Just get it over with."

I smeared and ripped her bright pink muff until the shape of a heart stood out. Whether because of errant tint or the aggravation of the waxing, the skin around the heart was almost as pink as the heart itself. I handed her a mirror and she held it over her new cha, inspecting my handiwork.

"The tint on your skin will go away in a day or two. You can use a little makeup or concealer tonight."

"Ohh, this looks nice," Natalie purred.

There was a big tip for me that day and hopefully some big tips for Natalie come Valentine's Day.

Later that evening, my husband and I sat down to eat dinner. The kids were at Grandma's, so we plunked down in front of the television. I had worked late so my husband had ordered pizza, his version of "cooking" dinner. He eyed me suspiciously while I folded the pizza piece in half and took a big bite.

"What?" I asked with eyebrows raised.

"Why are your fingers all pink?" he asked.

"Oh," I looked at my hands distractingly, forgetting they were pink, "Because Natalie the stripper came in today and had me dye her pubic hair pink for Valentine's Day," I said as I took a bite, shoving the stray strings of cheese back into my mouth, my eyes glued to some Food Network show.

"Don't you think you should wash your hands?" he asked, his face all scrunched up in a look of disgust.

"My hands are clean honey, just pink, I couldn't get the dye off."

"I don't know if I should be grossed out or turned on."

"It's just another day at work, babe. Some days I come home with a sore neck, some days I come home with pink fingers," I paused, "or pubic hair stuck to my shoe."

"You have pink fingers because you dyed some stripper's pubic hair pink–you know that's not a normal day at the office for most people, right?"

"Oh, and I waxed it into the shape of a heart," I added.

"That's really touching."

"Yes, there was touching involved, that's how my fingers got pink." I said. "Wouldn't it have been funny if I came home with pink dye all over my face," I teased.

"How did you do it?"

"I just bleached the crap out of it, then I frosted her with a little Manic Panic. Then I waxed that shit all pretty."

"And then you guys got totally naked and had a pillow fight until the feathers started flying out and then you got tired and snuggled right?" he offered wistfully.

"*No.*"

"Couldn't you just lie to me *once?*"

My husband would be even happier when he had the opportunity to see my work firsthand. You see, strippers are not the only contact I have had with the adult entertainment industry. Often I ask new clients toward the end of their wax if anyone else is going to appreciate my handiwork. It has been an effective way of skirting the 'are you gay or straight or cheating on your spouse' question and still get all the pertinent intel.

Usually the client will tell me about her boyfriend, girlfriend, husband or potential hookup. So imagine my surprise when I asked Darlene this same question and she informed me that my work would be appearing on film, uncredited of course.

"Huh? Wuh?" I was a little confused and she read it on my face.

"I'm doing a porn tomorrow," she said nonchalantly.

"Really?" I said, "*really?*"

I had pegged her as a possible stripper when she came in. She was tall, thin, with big fake boobs stretched unnaturally taut against her bony chest, Juicy Couture velour pants in cotton-candy pink, a nearly see-through wife beater, too much fake tan, a belly ring, a tongue ring, and a stumbly swagger from what seemed to be a creative cocktail of prescription meds.

Like I said, I have a pretty big roster of strippers. They are nice girls really, many of them somewhat broken, slightly lewd over-sharers. I'm not always right, but after waxing so many, I have a sense for these things. I can also spot the recently divorced woman edging her way back into the dating world, the married lady trying to spice things up a little and the woman who is on my table despite her reticence and fear because her mate suggested it.

I had seen so many different kinds of women, but this was my first adult-film actress. After I picked my jaw up off the floor, I had a million questions; she had offered the information, so I figured at this point there was very little verboten. Is this your first film? No. Have you been doing this for a while? Yes. What kind of films do you do? Oh, wow all that, hmm, what don't you do? Does *anyone* do that? What's your stage name? (Note to self to burn this into my memory so I can Google her later.) Does your family know? Do you like your job? What's it like? Are you enjoying yourself at all? Didn't think so. How much money do you make? That's it? Really? I thought it would be more.

She was very forthcoming. The only thing that threw me off was the next time she came in to get a facial, her murmurs of pleasure were just a little too orgasmic for my comfort. I didn't want any clients to hear her and think we offered a little extra if you just asked *real* nice.

And the answer is yes. Yes, I remembered her name. Yes, I did an unfiltered Google search for her. Yes, I watched the clip. Okay fine, I watched *all* the clips. Her enthusiasm for her job rivaled even my own, and I am a *dedicated* waxer. All I can say is, with my meticulous work, she was going to look even better in her *next* film.

....

SIX

NO GOOD, STINKY, HAIR-PANTS LADY

W hy out of all the wax joints, in all the towns, in all the world, did she walk into mine? Maybe she was part of an elaborate restitution scheme for some Karmic debt I owed. It could be repayment for the waitresses I stiffed as a miserly teenager. Was it for the hours I pilfered at my office job surfing the web and playing computer solitaire? Perhaps it was the universe bitch-slapping me for the cooking magazine I pilfered from my doctor's office just days before. I'm not sure, but someone, somewhere, was very mad at me.

She was smelly. She had fetid feet, putrid pits, a rank rump and a malodorous mound. The women I see are generally self-conscious about being clean and odor free. I put baby wipes in the bathroom because clients were rubbing their girl parts raw with the wood-pulp, paper towels afraid that being an hour out from their shower, they might have odor. This particular client, I will call her Susan (not a pseudonym, that's her *real* name), apparently did not share the same hygiene concerns.

Ripped

Susan had made an appointment for a slew of waxing services, which basically amounted to a full-body wax: legs, toes, cha-cha, backside, arms, underarms, brow, lip and chin. The only thing she *wasn't* waxing was her back, and truthfully, it could have used it. This woman was hairy– so hairy that when she took her pants off, it looked like she still had pants on, *hair* pants.

Susan was hairy like a hipster barista's beard. Hairy like Robin Williams' knuckles. She looked like she had smuggled Zach Galifianakis in her underpants. Had she been born a hundred years earlier, she would have had a long and illustrious career with the circus. Imagine how different the lives of the world's bearded ladies might have been had they had access to a talented waxer.

To further complicate things, she was a large woman and I had to put some real muscle into waxing her. Between her size and the profuseness of her monkey suit, I

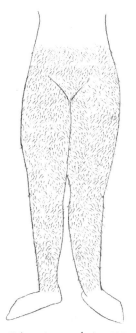

Hair pants are so last season.

used far more wax than is typical. She was stinky and hairy and a difficult case, but really, had she been a nice person, it wouldn't have mattered. But as I set about making her hair free, she seemed set on rubbing me the wrong way. After only ten minutes of conversation, I wanted to set myself on fire in protest. I don't mean she was just boring, though she was; she was tedious, obtuse, and lacking in any self-awareness. Several times during the service I had visions of stuffing a towel in her mouth until I was finished.

She told me about her dating woes, about how every guy she met was old and bald and fat and poor. Never mind *she* was fat and poor, still under the financial wing of her parents even though she was in her forties. She rambled on about her current fiancé, whom she had met in a chat room. She talked nonstop about how hot he was and how rich he was and how she was going to Vegas to meet him in person for the first time and get married. I resisted the impulse to tell her she was probably going to end up stuffed in a barrel somewhere in a rented storage unit. She went on *ad nauseum* and of course, the customer service-oriented professional that I am, I feigned interest over the almost *three hours* that I waxed her. I even asked her questions. What kind of wedding are you having? Have you picked out your dress?

Of course, giving any appearance of interest was a giant mistake because it opened the floodgates for her to spout more and more. When I was finally finished, ready for her to pay me and leave, she spent the next forty-five minutes talking about her forties-themed wedding, specifically her hairstyle. I'm not exaggerating, this woman spent forty-five of my minutes, the only time I had between clients in a ten-hour day on my feet—time I intended to sit down and eat lunch—explaining to me in minute detail how she was going to do her stinky hair. No matter how many times I stood up and walked toward the door, my subliminal way to politely tell clients it's time to go, she just sat there talking. I started opening and reading my mail, hoping *that* would send a message. No such luck.

Ripped

Finally, my telephone rang. It was a recorded telemarketer message.

"Oh, oh my gosh. Really?" I forced my face into a look of concern, "I'm sorry," I whispered to her pointing at the phone, "it's my six-year old's school on the phone, I need to take this. Congratulations and have fun." She looked confused as I waved and pointed at the door, "I'll see you next time." She finally left.

My waxing room was in shambles, the trash can was overflowing with gooey strips of muslin and sticky spatulas. I generally use the same sheet for the day, covering it with disposable paper sheets between clients but nothing was salvageable. I stripped the bed, emptied all the trash cans, restocked all the supplies I had gone through, and gave everything a generous wiping down before I finally scarfed down a few bites of my lunch and my next client came in.

So, a week later when Susan's check for nearly four-hundred dollars bounced, I came out of my skin. Now checks bounce, mistakes happen but I had already wasted too much time on this woman and now I was going to have to spend more chasing her down to get my money. I picked up the phone and got her right away.

"Hi Susan, it's Chris from the spa."

"Hi."

"I'm calling to let you know your check didn't go through."

Silence.

"Oh, yeah, I saw that." She said distracted.

Then why didn't *you* call *me*, I thought. "Well, I wanted to let you know."

"Uh, I can't come in and pay you right now because I'm not in town."

"That's okay Susan, I can run a credit card right over the phone and we'll be good to go." I said politely.

"I don't have a credit card."

Who the fuck over thirty doesn't have a credit card? "You *don't* have a credit card?" I asked.

"I get back on Tuesday and I can come in and give you a check."

Uh, lady, there is no way you can expect me to take another check from you after you bounced one, really? "I'll need cash or a credit card."

"Oh, well I'm really busy on Tuesday. I'm not sure if I'm going to have time to go to the bank."

Seriously? I thought. You bounce a check, make me wait a week and then you're not sure if you have the time to get cash? Fuck, you *make* time. I was silent.

"I'll try."

"Okay, I will see you Tuesday then."

Predictably, Tuesday came and went and no Susan. So, I called again Wednesday.

"Hi Susan, it's Chris from the spa."

"Oh hi." She said deflated.

"I'm calling because you told me you'd come by yesterday and pay me for the check you bounced."

"Oh yeah, I'm sorry. My car got broken into and they took my bag. It had all my stuff in it–my keys, ID, credit cards."

WAIT A FUCKING MINUTE, DID SHE JUST SAY CRED-
IT CARDS? "Susan, you told me last week you didn't *have* any
credit cards."

"Oh, uh uh," she stammered, "I meant my *debit* card."

"I can run debit cards too." I practically spat back at her.

"But I don't have it now because it was stolen," she volleyed
back at me.

"So what are you going to do?"

"Uh, I can come by on Friday after work and bring the money?"

"Okay, I will see you Friday."

Friday. No Susan. So I called her from the spa several times
Saturday, Sunday, and Monday with no luck, she was not even
answering her phone. On a hunch, I called her from my personal
cell phone rather than the recognizable spa number and, lo and
behold, she picked up on the first ring.

"Hello?"

"Hi Susan it's Chris calling from the spa." Ha!

"Uh, uh, uh, uh," she stammered, "hi?"

"I waited for you on Friday. What happened?"

"Oh, blah, blah, blah..." I can't even hear her now because the
blood rushing through my ears is deafening.

"Susan, I performed a service, I did a good job yes?"

"Yes."

"Not only have I not been paid for that service but I actually
had to pay twenty dollars in the form of a returned check fee for
the *pleasure* of waxing you."

"Uh, okay."

"So I would like you to fulfill your obligation and pay me the money you owe me."

"I could probably drop off money on Thursday."

"I will be here Susan, will you?"

"I'll see you Thursday." She couldn't get off the phone fast enough.

Again, Thursday came and went and it was about this time that I was pretty sure I was never going to see my money. I picked up my phone and called her.

"Blah, blah, leave a message, BEEP."

"Hi, Susan this is Chris, just sitting here waiting for my four-hundred dollars. Yeah, really wish I could go get groceries for my kids but well, guess that's not going to happen today. I sure hope you can find a way to be okay with the fact that you have taken food out of the mouths of my children. Okay, call me back." I left this message in my most sickeningly sweet, chirpy voice possible.

A few days later I picked up the phone again.

"Hi Susan, it's Chris, I just wanted to let you know that I really enjoyed waxing you the other week, thanks so much for letting me do that. Maybe we can do it again sometime, maybe you'll even let me buy you lunch afterward. Call me."

A few weeks after that, I picked up the phone again.

"Hi Susan, it's Chris at the spa, I was just having a rough day and thought maybe we could talk. Thanks for the ear. Yeah, this client of mine stiffed me on several hundred dollars and I'm really upset about it, oh wait that was you. Where's my money Stealy McStealerson?"

There were a few more phone calls like this, devolving into full-blown hostility on my part. She wouldn't pick up the phone after that, probably not for anybody. I left a message every few weeks for six months or so, and then buried her returned check with her number on it in the top drawer of my desk. Whenever I was having a particularly rough day, I would dig it out and make a phone call to blow off a little steam. I began to think of it as therapy.

If my husband had been distracted with me, Susan got a call. If my kids were acting up, I'd just ring up my friend Susan. Susan spared my loved ones from my PMS, my domestic frustrations and mood swings. In that way, she became very useful.

I finally threw the check away a year later. I didn't need it anymore. After that long, I felt like I had more than gotten my four-hundred dollars' worth. Karma–it's relative. Who knows? Maybe Susan is out there somewhere writing a story right now about how this crazy Brazilian waxer message-stalked her for almost a year.

....

SEVEN

BEAUTY & THE BUTT

f I had a hidden camera capturing what clients did in the moments to themselves in the changing room before I began the waxing service, I'm certain I would find most of them giving their girl bits a once over with the baby wipes. Let me just take a moment to reassure my past, present, and future clients that I have never, at any time, had a hidden camera in the wax room, though a webcam certainly would have been a great way to pay the bills during the lean years. That hidden camera thing is just a *hypothetical* scenario and probably a bad one. Anyhow, I leave a box of unscented baby wipes in the changing room so clients don't try to tidy up their business using the rough, woody paper towel I use to dry my hands after washing them. There's nothing like starting a Brazilian and the client's cha-cha looks something like a black sweater washed with a Kleenex, all sorts of little tissue balls stuck everywhere. In between clients, if I have time, I like to empty the trash inside the changing room—just makes things look and feel fresh for the next customer. In doing so I have noticed people's proclivity for the wipes. Some women are one wipers, a quick once over to refresh, to double check, just in case. Some are two wipers, conceivably one wipe for the front and one for the back, keeping things separate but equal. A few clients use three or more wipes, probably in an effort to clean what they view to be a dirty, smelly, embarrassing shame-hole. If you are that dirty, perhaps a shower would be more efficient, no? Now that I think about it, it is *possible* that keeping such close tabs, albeit unintentionally, on how many ass wipes another person uses is just as creepy as the hidden camera that I *don't* have.

While I may have an unnatural fixation on other peoples' baby-wipe use, many women do seem to have some pretty entrenched ideas about smelly vaginas. I have a few clients, always female, who will use perfume to effectively *Febreze* their lady business. I'm going to go out on a limb and say it–it is probably always a bad idea to spritz your vag with anything named Poison, Opium or Impulse (*The body spray with the reassurance of deodorant!* That's actually its tagline). If a complete stranger suddenly gives you flowers, it's probably because he feels bad that you sprayed your vagina with chemicals. These complicated stink eradicating rituals are entirely unnecessary. It is perfectly okay that a vagina smell like a vagina and not like coconuts or lavender. Ladies, save the glitter and litany of Bath and Body Works bursting berries coochie spray for your big Saturday night. For my comfort and yours, just be showered that same day and if it's late in the day, give yourself a once over with a wipe. Thankfully, just as I brush my teeth and refrain from eating poppy seed bagels or Oreos before my dentist appointments, most women show up for their waxing appointment in a state of mother-in-law visiting cleanliness, shipshape and ready for the white-glove test. And while stinky vaginas are rarely a problem, dirty and stinky feet, on the other hand, are at near *epidemic* levels.

The official state shoe of Southern California is the flip-flop. I'm pretty sure that is a real fact because I read it on the Internet. I have seen way more than my fair share of seriously filthy feet. Forget grey tootsies with a little dirt or fuzz clinging to them and think ink black soles that look like they belong to a barefoot coal miner—the kind of dirt that must be removed with a pumice stone and a strong arm rather than a wash cloth and soap. Perhaps surprisingly, dirty feet don't gross me out, but I *have* seen a couple of freakishly disconcerting hammertoes. Women who wear those crazy Kardashian, stacked, platform-stiletto heels seriously have the ugliest, mangled, hobbit-looking feet. Listen ladies, feet are like teeth–really nice to have–right? Knock it off with the barbaric heels already or you'll have to Louboutin the underside of your wheel chair someday. While dirty and gnarled feet don't bother me too much, I have a tough time with smelly feet. Women, in all of their sweetness and light can still produce some of the mightiest foot stink ever. This is probably because so many women wear uncomfortable, tight-fighting, often synthetic shoes that do not breathe, coupled with no socks to absorb perspiration. I have one client that has such rank feet that she brings little socks to put on just during the wax to contain her foot stink. Unfortunately, her shoes still reek so bad that just sitting there unoccupied, they fill the room with noxious vapor reminiscent of very bad takeout or very good cheese.

Dirty feet and funky toes aside, most of my clients are careful groomers. Generally women who are keen to get each and every pube removed are equally detailed in all areas of their girly maintenance. Still, there have been a few dirty vaginas. (I was going to write a *handful* of dirty vaginas but that brings to mind a really disturbing image.) I have seen ladies who seem to need a lesson on moving their bits and bobs around a little and degunkifying things. When faced with a client who is producing her own artisanal cheese, my usual meticulousness is quickly abandoned. I simply do a quicky and boot her out the door. I figure if she won't get in there and clean under the hood, I am off the hook. Hampered-hygiene clients get wise and either tidy up better or stop coming in, either of which works for me.

Speaking of noxious vapors, occasionally I will encounter a client with a very strong butt smell. Not poop stink, mind you, just noticeable pheromones. I have become accustomed to it, as much as one can become accustomed to the smell of another person's butt in close proximity. Most of the time it doesn't faze me. Most jobs don't come with an array of odors that you have to live with, but my job certainly isn't the only one. My guess is dentists probably smell a lot of bad breath and bra fitters probably smell a lot of body odor and kindergarten teachers probably smell a lot of poop. I take some small comfort that I am not alone in this vocational olfactory stink cloud. When I was pregnant, I smelled things on a whole new level—it was like superhero level enhanced senses. Every odor asserted itself boldly and even nice smells would trigger a wave of nausea so strong which, if not immediately countered with fresh air, would lead to some midday heaving. In the throes of pregnancy sensitivity, it seemed as if *everyone* had a stinky butt. If I were to pause in the middle of a Brazilian wax to go into the bathroom to throw up in high volume (the only way I throw up) I would have lost a lot of clients. I had to protect my delicate senses surreptitiously. When I got to the butt part of the waxing service, I would step away from the client, smile and take a very deep, but quiet breath, hold it and finish off the bum. Of course I had to do this casually and unobtrusively. No one wants you to exaggeratedly try *not* to smell their butt. Most of us women are self-conscious enough without adding new things about our bodies to feel anxious about.

Some women get really self-conscious about their butts. They could be all chill about me waxing their cha, seeing every knob and flap. But the butt? Pure humiliation. Maybe because it's the business end, maybe they have some sort of lingering Freudian butt angst. Maybe these butt-bashful babes think back to the last time they pooped and are replaying it in their minds, hoping they wiped well enough. You know how you wipe different when you think someone else is going to be around there versus when you know you are getting in the shower in a few minutes? Maybe they worry that in the unconscious routine that wiping is, that perhaps they forgot that they had to wipe for *company*. I don't know. Yes, I have seen some missed poop here and there. Shit happens is not just a cliché, it really *happens*, people.

When I tell women to pull their legs toward their chest, it's time to wax their bum, I get one of two responses. They either groan, "I'm so embarrassed" or "Uh, no, *I* don't have any hair back there." The thing is, if you have seen one butt, you've pretty much seen them all. The chas all look a little different, but buttholes all pretty much look the same.

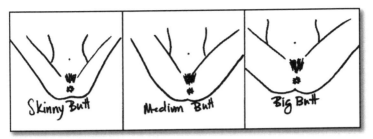

It was always when I was working on one of my sketches for the book that one of my kids would come in and ask, "Mom, what are you doing?" with a screwed-up look on their face. I'm pretty sure my youngest told her preschool class, when asked what I do for a living, "Oh, my mom draws butts all day."

Sure I have seen a hemorrhoid here and there, but that's about as exciting as it gets. And as far as butt hair is concerned, believe me, you have some. We all do. Butt hair is universal. The lucky girls have the fine down or a few stragglers, and the unlucky females have hair panties. I have long hair (on my head, not on my butt, not that there is anything wrong with really long butt hair– that is, if it is on someone other than me) and when I wash my hair, the shed hair will rinse out of my head and some of it will collect in the crack of my bum. So at the end of every shower, I have to go grab the hair in my bum lest it give me itchy butt all day. That's how I know when it's time to wax my bum, when I go for a grab and the hair is attached.

Ripping the hair from your bum is actually the least painful part of the Brazilian wax. Perhaps psychologically painful for those who have anxiety over me getting a close-up of their anus, but from a strictly physical side, it's less uncomfortable. The bum does, however, seem more sensitive to heat. Clients always note that the wax I have used for the entire procedure becomes magically hotter when placed directly beside their bum hole. "What are you, singeing them?" they'll ask me. "Oh pipe down," I will tell them, "I'm the one picking the last remnant of wax off your winker."

I have seen butts of many colors and from all over the world. I have wiped them with little antiseptic towels. I have powdered them. I have wiped oil across them in pre-wax preparation. I have slathered them in wax. I have smoothed muslin strips over a sea of butt cheeks and then ripped the hair from these same butts. I have gingerly dabbed them with post-wax balm. Given the close proximity to buttholes that is part and parcel of this job, I've gotten over any shyness I might have had about touching strangers. You simply cannot be in this business if you have an aversion to buttholes. I'm not bragging, but I have touched a *lot* of butts in my day. You know, I *would* like to brag about it because I do not know a single person who has touched as many butts as I have. Is there some kind of J.D. Power's award for that? Because if there is, I have it *nailed*. Let's just say I work with a lot of assholes, but if you take a look at how many assholes you work with, my guess is, you have me beat.

....

EIGHT

VAJARGON: A FEW WORDS
ABOUT WORDS

For many years, I have used vagina improperly. Not that I have been using *my* vagina improperly mind you. Or anyone else's for that matter. At least I don't *think* so. How does one misuse a vagina anyhow? I bet R. Kelly knows. What I mean is that I have been using the *word* vagina incorrectly. Many people are unaware that the area that I wax is not actually called the vagina. I myself have said things like "I am so tired of looking at vaginas," after a long Friday schedule full of Brazilian waxing clients. I have assured nervous first-timers, "I promise not to wax your vagina off." I have said to my assistant on more than one occasion, "if you need me, I'll be in the wax room waxing my vag, so don't bug me unless it's important." I have lamented to my husband during the economic downturn, "well, at least the vagina waxes will keep us in groceries."

Vagina actually refers to a polluted canal in Venice. Wait, that's not right. The vagina is a "fibro muscular, tubular tract leading from the uterus to the exterior of the body in female placental mammals and marsupials, or to the cloaca in female birds, monotremes, and some reptiles." How is that for technical? What did we ever do before Wikipedia, right? To simplify, the vagina is the canal, the vulva is what is outside. Also, after much spell checking and meticulously combing several sources–okay, mostly Wikipedia and an online dictionary–I found that the plural of vagina is not exclusively the *vaginas* I frequently use, but also vaginae. I love to pepper my speech with neologisms and obscure variants of words, so I can't wait to pull out vaginae. Lord knows this job will provide ample opportunity. Translated from its origin word, vagina means "cave of mystery." I think cave of mystery is kind of a nice description, although *Vagina: Cave of Mystery* does sound like an episode of Scooby Doo. Like some snaggle-toothed old caretaker, or perhaps my husband, is going to say, if it weren't for you meddling kids, I would have gotten into the Cave of Mystery.

I discovered while researching words that Google herself is a real prudy bitch. I would start typing in *vagina* and Google would be like, *v-a-*, ah, are you looking for *vacation rentals*? No, how about *vasculitis*, no? I would continue, *v-a-g*, and Google would step in, ah Chris is it *vagabond*? Is that it? Perhaps *vagus nerve*, no? I would get further, *v-a-g-i*, and Google would abruptly clam up like, uh, Chris, really, I have no idea where you are going with this and, frankly, I am a little surprised that you are trying to make me search for a you-know-what. Maybe Google is channeling my mother. Of course, when I finally get all the words in and hit search, Google complied and gave me my search information, but it was pretty clear that she wasn't going to do me any favors.

While I was clearing up all this vagina business, I came across a nifty online pronunciation guide. There is no shortage of opportunities at distraction and procrastination when you are trying to write a book. This pronunciation guide was a useful way to both amuse myself and irritate my husband in our small, shared office. My computer would announce in a monotonous, robotic voice, "*Vagina, from the Latin vaginum for sheath, va-gi-na, vagina, diminutive vaginum,...*"

"What is that?" my husband asked, turning around both interested and irritated.

"Nothing honey, just working on my book," I answered dismissively like I was engrossed in very important work.

"*Mitte gladium in vaginam, translated as, put the sword into its sheath.*"

"Knock it off with the dirty Speak and Spell, I'm trying to work."

"Me too. Sometimes it's hard to share an office. Deal. I don't get mad when you have to do your software engineerdy stuff."

"That's different, I'm not saying *vagina, vagina, vagina* while you try and get your work done."

"It's not my fault that your job isn't as interesting as mine," I countered. "Now stop talking to me, I am *trying* to write."

"*Vagina, vagina, vagina, vagina.* See? It's distracting, isn't it?"

I pointedly ignored him and continued to click away at the computer, engaged in the serious and important work of chronicling a bunch of stories about genital waxing.

So if *vagina* isn't really accurate, what is the *correct* terminology? The area that I wax, or the female genitalia as a whole, not *hole*, is more accurately referred to as the *vulva*. I am about one-hundred percent sure that in all of the years I have been waxing, I have never told a woman that I was about to wax her vulva. I have also not said, what shape do you desire on your vulva today? Or even, would you like to go completely bare on your vulva? For whatever reason, *vagina* has stepped in to substitute in common parlance for the seldom-used *vulva*. So while calling the general area your *vagina* might be incorrect, it appears to be what the ladies prefer, at least on the more technical side. Most of the time, however, I use one of the many permutations possible. I have an ample supply of pussy patois and vagina vernacular. I refer to this collection of slang and euphemisms as *vajargon*, the vocabulary particular to Brazilian waxers.

The first of these came of course, from my family. My mother used the shame-laced *your you-know-what*, as in "I told my friend Rita about how you wax *your you-know-what* and she said she thought only strippers did that." My grandmother, who chronically mispronounces words like *nuclear* and *counselor* and *library* and *jewelry*, speaks of one's *virg-eye-na*, like a meld of the words *virgin* and *vagina*. If anyone else in our family utters *virg-eye-na*, it is instantly clear to the rest of us that my grandmother is being made fun of. *Virg-eye-na* works well to conjure up old timey country songs like the hit, *I Left My Virg-eye-na in Virginia*. I've also heard from both my mother and my grandma the words that hold the vagina and vulva up in all of its beautiful female glory, *down there*. "*Down there?*" I would ask my mother, "You mean like Australia?" Again, *down there* is too shaming for me. I have never once told my daughters to wash *down there* or not to touch *down there*. It makes it seem like some impossibly unknowable and confusingly vague place. In our house we say *vagina* and *gina* and yes, even *cha-cha*. I will always fondly remember my youngest daughter as a toddler running around the house naked after her bath, smacking her crotch like bongo drums shouting," I slappa my cha-cha, I slappa my cha-cha." Or the girls repeating the stranger danger talks I gave them to my mortified mother-in-law, "we only touch our *own* ginas, Gramma, no one else can touch ours," offered my seven-year-old. "But we can touch our own," my youngest piped in happily. Good times.

I also pull out euphemisms based on my perceptions of the client. For my epicureans and chef-types, *mango* works very well, one fleshy, sweet fruit standing in for the other. For my animal lovers, *kitty* is colloquial, like "let's get those whiskers off your kitty." For the military types, I find *privates* works well and I even offer the standard new recruit crew cut for women who want easy wash, low-maintenance without going fully bald. Military and police types also respond well to the no-nonsense *vag*, probably because it sounds like *badge*. For my Latinas, *pudenda* is preferred (Latin for shame by the way). For the rednecks it's cooter and for the Mormons I refer to it as one's *babymaker* or *sister-wife*. For my clients over fifty, *lady business* sums it up and adds a little class. My sports enthusiasts have *honeymoon tackle* and my Catholics have a *shame-hole*. For my Brits, *fanny* is both light and accurate. To refer to the female sex as *goodies* sounds like a present— it's exciting. And of course for the purists and etymologists among my clientele, there is always *vulva*. There are more still, like your *nether regions, vajayjay, snatch, punani* and *hoo-ha*. For my dance enthusiasts, there is the *cha-cha*, probably my most used. There is *bush*, for Republicans of course. Then there are *coochie, giner*, and your *little lady*. I don't generally use neologisms that refer to it as a receptacle, but I could get behind the spectacular *receptacular*. For my hip-hop fans, the Notorious *V.A.G.* gives the vagina some much-needed street cred.

There are of course, words I never use with a client. I find the *bald man in a boat* vague and too wordy—sounds like a Hemingway or Steinbeck novel. Besides the lovely *mango*, food comparisons are generally a no-no. You will never hear me say *pink taco, bearded clam, bikini biscuit, furburger, vertical bacon sandwich, hair pie* or even *beef curtains*. While *kitty* is ok, *pussy* is just rude. I might use this on my own, but never to a client. Also off limits is anything that compares the lovely thing between one's legs to a *wound*. I don't use *muff* or *panty hamster* or *wunder down under*. There are of course, no references made to size. No one has a *Grand Canyon*, a *Great Divide* or a *Mariana's Trench*. Likewise, I never remove a woman's *brillo pad* or rid her of her *baby bear* or wax her *camel toe*.

Interestingly enough, I don't have a similar array of vocabulary for the male genitalia. Only a fraction of my Brazilian wax clients are male but it surprises even me that I haven't developed a similar set of penis parlance and testicle terminology. I thought back to how I refer to the male sex as I wax and I found I usually don't refer to it as *anything*. Rather, I refer around it. Usually I will say *yourself*, as in "cover yourself with this." Or *here*, like, "put your hand here for me and pull upwards so I can finish up." I have also heard many a Brazilian waxer refer to it as *junk*. For example, "Yeah, I wax guys but they have to hold their own junk." *Junk*, it sounds like something you keep around and haven't managed to get rid of because you might need it someday, but probably not. Apt descriptions of some husbands no? I have referred to the male Brazilian as a *back, sac and crack* or *twigs and berries* but only between waxers for our own amusement, never to a client.

Much like the idea that Eskimos have an unusually large number of words that in some way mean snow, we have so many words that reference vagina that one can glean its overall cultural importance. Language shapes how we feel about ourselves and it gives us the vocabulary to talk about our bodies, sexual health, and sexual desire. Linguists suggest that when we have all these neologisms, it highlights a gap in the popular discourse. So many of the words we use to describe the female sex are misogynistic or at the very least, describe the vagina from the male point of view. Do we have enough words that are not coy, clinical or crude? It is somewhat concerning that so many ways of talking about female genitalia reference shame and embarrassment.

While there is an undercurrent of female genital shame that runs through our culture, there appears to be a seemingly universal male-genital pride. Men are so enamored of their own organs–always looking at them, checking to make sure they're still there, moving them around from one side to another, even smacking them against things for no reason other than their own amusement.

VAJARGON: A FEW WORDS ABOUT WORDS

Would a woman ever grab her labia, stretch them out like a mouth and manipulate them like a puppet, giving them their own voice? I just can't see a woman doing this, but I can totally see a guy doing nearly the same thing. In fact, I *have* seen it done. Men love their junk and prove it by the delight they take in walking around naked and whacking their manhood against things like the cat, the piano and even resting it on their wife's head as she lays in bed trying to write her masterpiece and make them ten-thousandaires.

NINE

....

ELEPHANT EARS

"You know, if there were anything to this whole *Secret*, manifest your dreams by thinking about something and imagining yourself already having it thing, a lot more fifteen-year-old boys would be having awkward sex with Norwegian super models," my husband remarked.

His negative attitude was understandable given that I had just pulled him from a very important Star Trek video game mission to watch *The Secret* with me and, uh, I don't know, plan the fulfillment of our combined *destinies*. "Don't worry honey," I had told him, "it's just my dreams. No go on, keep playing your video game." He had finally agreed to watch with me after I promised popcorn and refreshments.

"You're probably right," I said watching him try to get popcorn into his mouth, "if there were something to the *Secret*, the whole dream it, see it, be it, I'd already be frolicking on a beach somewhere in Capri with Liam Neeson."

"*Ouch.* You know you already have every fifteen-year-old boy's dream job, right? Loads of naked, spread-eagled women on your table each day..." I watched my husband slowly drift to his personal happy place.

How did I land a fifteen-year-old boy's dream job? I'd rather have a thirty-six-year-old woman's dream job—you know, professional Bravo watcher and shoe shopper—but at least my job is envy-inducing for someone. Every time I'm in a mixed group and people find out what I do for a living, at least one guy will pipe in, "Uh, well if you ever need an assistant, har, har, sign me up," while his wife shoots imaginary daggers at his head. I hear this line so often that my husband and I will actually wager on which guy will say it first.

It's true, more women have spread their legs for me in a professional capacity than for Charlie Sheen. They do it willingly, without drinks, dinner or a mountain of cocaine and then they pay *me* for the pleasure. The upside of all of the vag I see on such a regular basis is that I have become very comfortable with the female body, including my own. Pap smear? Yes please! My doctor wants her medical students to lend a hand? No problem, I don't give it a second thought. When I am waxing a client, all I see is hair that they want removed. Whether it's an underarm, a brow or a bum makes very little difference. In fact, an eyebrow wax is a more difficult wax in some ways because it requires a high degree of artistry whereas a full monty cha-cha wax just requires a certain attention to detail. My work at the spa has put me into contact with scores of naked women. During the average Brazilian wax I get to see bellies, butts, thighs, legs and of course, vaginas exposed under bright lights, sometimes under a magnified lamp to tweeze the last few stragglers. Seeing such a wide cross section of women has made me realize that we are exposed to so many airbrushed and retouched images that we forget what women's bodies *really* look like.

With the sole exception of the local university girls' swim team, who truly had the most beautiful bodies I have ever seen–an amazing combination of strength and shape–every woman I've worked on has cellulite. In fact, skinny girls who don't work out seem to get it the worst. Every naked body that has rested on my table has veins mapping the circulatory system. I have seen scarred knees and stretch marks, some from children borne, some from weight lost, others from growth spurts. I have seen scary dark wiry hairs that shoot from all manner of seemingly unfair places like the back of our legs or even our nipples. I have seen navels stretched from childbirth and scars from ingrown hairs. I have seen dimpled knees and pimpled butts. I've witnessed mastectomy scars, broken noses healed over in the aftermath of being beaten by an abusive spouse and more C-section scars than I can count. I've noted the strangely taut skin from oversized breast implants put into too small a woman. I've seen scars from accidents, attacks and surger-ies. I've seen tattoos, some cherished by their owners, others loathed.

I don't judge and I don't look at bodies with the appraising eye of an art collector, more matter-of-factly, like a mother cleaning up her toddler. As a rule, I also don't talk smack about my clients or reveal their secrets. I am told about affairs, sob stories and so many secret, private things that I consider myself to have some-thing akin to a doctor-patient privilege. The vulnerability of the service has given me a great respect for clients, their bodies and their privacy. But there was this *one* time...

I started having occasional spa parties in the evenings and on Sundays when we would normally be closed. It was a great way to boost revenue and introduce new customers to our services. Birthdays, bridal showers, and low-key bachelorette parties were the most common. Zoe, a favorite client of mine, inquired about having her bachelorette party at the spa. She was very close with her sister, a Mormon, and while there could be drinking and general girl buffoonery, she didn't want anything in the way of plastic penises or strippers. So we arranged for light catering, champagne and flowers in her wedding colors. I had an abbreviated service menu the women could choose from and swag they could take home. The maid-of-honor paid for the drinks and food and the mother-of-the-bride graciously stepped in and paid for one high-end service for each attendee. The girls could have a massage, a pedicure, a facial or a bikini wax. They could also upgrade the service or pay for added smaller services on their own, like a brow wax or manicure. We had five technicians and about twelve partygoers so the girls took turns getting their services while the others drank, ate and celebrated Zoe's upcoming nuptials.

The crowd was a mix of friends and family. Everyone looked excited as they sipped their cocktails and picked their services for that evening. For many of the women, this was the first time they had been to a spa. I worked quickly to coordinate who would go where and when so that we could accommodate each person's requests. A few of the women went off for the first of their services. Others were picking out their manicure colors when *she* walked in. She was Margo, well she was Margo according to her driver's license but *Margaux* according to her. The pretentious French spelling she chose to use was apt. She strode in on gazelle legs, all stylish like she just stepped out of French Vogue. She was beautiful, stunning really, all shiny hair and enviably high cheekbones. She sat down between the girls, her long legs angled gracefully to the side like a resting show horse. The amiable hum of conversation stopped and you could almost feel the room drop in temperature. Margaux absentmindedly picked at some grapes and looked around with the expression of a queen who just woke up to find herself in a barn.

Zoe came into the room, having just finished the first of her services and saw Margaux had arrived. She gave her a quick hug and told her she was glad she could make it. I found out later that Margaux was the daughter of Zoe's mom's best friend and so the two had moved from childhood playmates to an adult version of Israel/Palestine in that although they didn't like or trust each other, their proximity forced them to honor an uneasy truce peppered by verbal missiles lobbed at each other now and then.

While absentmindedly thumbing through a magazine, Margaux prattled off the services she wanted. I spent a few minutes trying to move things around to fit her requests in. She had quite the list considering she seemed less than excited about the surroundings.

"What kind of wax do you use Clare?"

"It's Chris," I said politely," and I use both hard wax and soft wax, switching between the two depending on the service."

"I only use hard wax on my brows." She said, never looking up from the magazine.

"I prefer it as well."

"Do you do a lot of brows, because I am *very* particular?" Margaux whined.

"Well, every esthetician has his or her own style but I try very hard to understand what each client prefers and I translate that into a great brow. I am considered an expert when it comes to brow shaping. However, if you want to wait to see your usual person, I completely understand."

"No, you should be fine." She said flatly. "For the manicure, I need your nail lady to know that I don't like my cuticles cut, no cutting, just pushed back."

"When you are in with our manicurist, Cam, let her know your preferences and she will do whatever you need."

"Does she speak English?" she sighed, looking slightly exasperated.

Wow, this was getting better and better by the moment. I disliked Margaux but I was nice, I'm *always* nice. I may not like the client, but I always get along with their money. More girls came in the main room as others went off to get their services. The bride was sipping her drink and looking around, I was refilling glasses and answering questions and Margaux was busy making everyone uncomfortable.

The bride's mom tried to engage Margaux in conversation. "You should see Zoe's dress. It is so beautiful. I wasn't sure at first because of course, I had my own ideas but really, it's quite stunning."

"I have a picture on my phone if you'd like to see," Zoe offered excitedly.

"Sure," replied Margaux indifferently.

Margaux leaned forward and peered at Zoe's phone, eyes squinting and lips showing just the faintest curl of a grimace. "Mmmm, so pretty. What are you wearing with it?"

74

Ripped

Zoe eyed her mother with a warm smile, "My mother *finally* gave me my great grandmother's sapphire earrings. They are these pretty little flower clusters and I figured they are my something borrowed, something blue, and something old."

"Let me see the dress again," Margaux said with a hint of concern pulling Zoe's phone toward her with her spidery fingers.

Zoe seemed surprised that Margaux wanted a second look.

"Oh, no. You can't wear studs, they won't work with the neckline of your dress," Margaux said, pushing the phone back towards Zoe.

"Really?" asked Zoe, her face instantly deflated.

"See, your dress is really rather modern and your grandmother's old-fashioned earrings while, uh, *charming*, don't go with the dress. What that dress needs is some chandelier earrings. You're wearing your hair down, right?"

"Well, no, actually I was going to wear it up. I thought that would be the most elegant," Zoe said.

"No, no, no," Margaux said, with all the warmth of Anna Wintour. "You need to wear your hair down and chandelier earrings. The dress requires nothing less."

"I was hoping to make my great grandmother a part of the ceremony in some way plus we are kind of tapped out on spending, I don't have the budget for more jewelry."

"Here is what you do," Margaux said as if it was a foregone conclusion, "Get the dress, take it down to Saks and they will pull a few earrings for you that fit the dress," she said waving her hands like hauling a heavy expensive wedding dress to a store at the eleventh hour is the easiest thing in the world. "At most the earrings will run two hundred bucks or so. It's just costume jewelry."

Now, I am no fashion expert, but I do know one thing: you should never tell a bride what to do. Don't tell her anything she is doing is *wrong* or *unfashionable* and do not rain on her great grandma's sapphire-earring parade. Really, what is the point? Maybe the dress would look better with different hair or earrings, maybe the fashionable and French-Voguey Margaux was right. So what? Who told this woman it was her job to rid the world of poor dress/earring pairings?

Zoe looked upset and her mom, Bonnie, was speechless. I could almost see Bonnie simmering. Here was Margaux enjoying an evening at the spa at her expense while telling her daughter that her many-times-mulled-over choices were wrong.

Thankfully, Zoe's close friend piped in, "I think the earrings are perfect and a special way to have your great grandma there in spirit. You wore them at your wedding too, right Bonnie?" she asked Zoe's mother.

"Yes, I did."

"Then there you go, what a wonderful tradition," she said as she shot a look in Margaux's direction.

"Hmmm, your call I suppose," said Margaux.

"Margaux, why don't we do your brows now," I offered, trying to redirect things.

"Okay," she said unenthusiastically.

I sat her in the brow station chair looking at her, wondering how such a pretty face sat atop such a sour girl. I trimmed, waxed and bewitched her brows into gorgeous submission. They looked perfect and truthfully, she was such a stunning woman that her beauty made my work look even better.

"All done," I said cheerfully and handed her the mirror.

"Hmmm," she said, inspecting her brow with her face expressionless.

Unbelievable. My work was impeccable. I had purposefully been on my A game, knowing Margaux's critical eye would be hunting for mistakes.

"I think I see a few hairs over here," she said stroking her long, thin finger against her perfect, poreless temple.

I desperately wanted to *accidentally* pinch Margaux with my tweezers or drip a little wax straight through the middle of her well-groomed brows, leaving them looking like Vanilla Ice's.

But I didn't. Instead, I pretended to tweeze these invisible hairs, handed her the mirror again.

"Better?"

"Much," she said appraising herself in the mirror. She lifted herself off the chair without as much as a thank you.

"Mmm, Clare, can I get a Brazilian while I'm here?"

First of all, the name is *Chris*. Second, I was now redeemed because when clients refuse to give a compliment but want me to do something else, that's how I know they liked it. Ha, I win.

"*Margaret* let me see if I can move things around a bit." That's right, if you don't know my name then I don't know yours either. Although I was already feeling like I wanted less time with Margaux not more, the Brazilian was an extra sixty plus tip and Margaux was not likely to make an appointment for another time. I did some rearranging that didn't put anyone out and found a slot for Margaux's cha wax.

"Back here, follow me," I said, ushering her to the waxing room.

"Are we leaving anything behind, or taking it all?" I asked.

"Take everything."

I would be saying "Take everything, *please*" if someone were about to be near my girl business with hot wax but I am a mostly nice person and Margaux is not.

"In that case, it's easiest for me if you are naked from the waist down. You should be on the table face up, put your bum right here," I said pointing to the middle of the bed, "your feet right about here. There are wipes over there if you want to freshen up and you can hang up your clothes or rest them on that chair. Do you have any questions?"

"No."

"Then I will step out and let you get undressed, I'll be back in a few minutes and I will knock before I enter."

"Mmm-hmm."

I closed the door behind me and went into the break room where I found Jen, my massage therapist taking a quick breather.

"Are you working on someone?" she asked.

"I'm about to do a wax on Margaux."

"Lucky you."

"I know right? She is *not* a very nice girl."

"Yeah, I did a foot and leg massage on her. I don't even think she liked it, hard to tell. She has perfect legs though."

"I know. Please tell me she has ugly feet, an extra toe, bunions, corns or something?"

"No, they are perfect too."

Ripped

"Life isn't fair. I'll be done in about twenty and we can wrap it up and shoo everyone out. I better go."

"Okay. Have fun with that."

"Yay for me," I replied sarcastically, shaking imaginary pompoms while I headed back to the room.

I knocked softly. "Are you ready?"

"Yes," she answered.

I entered the room and closed the door behind me. Margaux lay on the bed, long legs together, perfect toes pointed. It was hard not to take note of her smooth olive skin, slender thighs and flat stomach. Some girls just win the genetics lottery.

After finishing up Margaux's wax, I settled up with the girls and Bonnie, Zoe's mother. I made Zoe's appointment for her pre-wedding makeup trial and final Brazilian just before the wedding and honeymoon. I hugged Zoe goodbye and shut the door behind the last of the partygoers.

Jennifer came in and slumped on a chair. The other staff were already sitting down, picking at the leftover food and finishing the near-empty bottle of champagne. "Well, that was fun," she said.

"Yes, it was. I'm just figuring out your totals, if you guys can wait a few minutes, I'll pay you tonight."

"Bonnie tipped well," I noted, adding up the service and tip totals.

"She was really nice. She talked to me while I did her nails and she was very happy with the party, Chris," said Cam, my quiet, polite, diminutive Cambodian manicurist.

"I'm glad she was pleased. Everyone seemed happy with their services," I said.

"Almost everyone," Jennifer piped in.

"Oh, you mean the giant woman? The tall skinny one? I don't like her, her face looked like she ate something sour," said Cam, who never had anything negative to say about anyone.

"Yeah, what was her problem, anyhow? How can someone so perfect be so miserable?" one of the other therapists asked.

"Oh, she's not perfect," I said baiting them.

"Well not perfect, but you know, she is *really* pretty," Jennifer said.

"Did you hear the stuff she was saying to Zoe?" asked Cory our other manicurist. "I thought Zoe's friend was going to haul off and smack a bitch."

"Margaux's pretty, but she's not pretty everywhere," I said, casting the line out further.

"What do you mean?" Jennifer turned and looked at me, knowing there was only one area of Margaux I saw that she hadn't.

"I began the wax like I always do, bending Margaux's leg to the side like a flamingo," I paused for effect, " when suddenly, the Earth changed its rotation, day turned night and the cosmic order of things blissfully righted itself."

The girls continued to munch on crackers and Brie, washing it down with the occasional sip of flat champagne, but they stopped chatting and turned their attention to me.

"There between her perfect legs was what I can best describe as," I paused, "elephant ears."

As the staff cringed in silence, I described her outer labia, "there was so much *there*, they were so *long*, that she probably had to roll them up to tuck them into her undies, although there was enough flesh that in would look like she was packing some serious junk. Everything was a grayish pink, like week-old, overcooked pork chops, well week-old overcooked *hairy* pork chops. I'm not kidding, it looked like she was smuggling bats in her pants. Her labia reminded me of my friend's mean old Basset hound's floppy ears. They were wrinkled and deflated looking and lord, I aspire to admire the range of differences in the female body but these lips were seriously the ugliest thing I had ever seen."

"Was it really that bad?" asked Jennifer, after dry heaving a little.

"I *tried* not to stare. I tried not to snicker and look away embarrassed. I resisted the impulse to pull her lips out to measure their wingspan." I pantomimed pulling giant wings out to my side like unfurling a cape.

Cam put her hand over her open mouth, "Oh Chris, you are *soooo* bad."

"I tried not to whip out a camera, snap a pic and send it to Ripley's Believe It or Not, Guinness World Records or at *least* TMZ. Instead, I did what I always do, I gave her a professional and thorough wax. But that," I paused, "that was the *ugliest* vagina I have ever seen."

Jennifer grimaced. "You're just saying that to make us feel better."

"No, I am telling the absolute truth. The junk she's smuggling in her front trunk is probably the reason she's such a bitch."

"If I had elephant ears, I'd be sour too," Cam added.

"They were so big, if she was boinking some guy, she could pull her lips around him like a blanket."

"Like a human *Snuggie!*" Jennifer said. Now we were just having fun.

I looked around the room at my staff, captivated by my tale like a bunch of Girl Scouts gathered around a campfire listening to scary tales and I was reminded that sometimes the worst clients make for the best stories.

TEN

....

THE ACCIDENTAL BRAZILIAN

Some of my clients come to me as seasoned waxers. Some are waxing virgins who start with a modest, edge of the leg bikini wax and work their way to the Brazilian as they become more comfortable with the process and, no doubt, more comfortable with me. Some newbies wanted it all off from the get go, and some Brazilians were purely accidental. How does one have an accidental Brazilian? Did a wax pot go flying, splashing wax all over some hapless women's pudenda? In my case, the accidental Brazilian happened because I got confused.

Nina was in her early forties, somewhat reserved, shy and newly single after a long, drawn out, painful divorce. She had been coming to me for facials to clear up a case of adult hormonal/stress/ex-husband acne and as she began dating again, she had expressed some curiosity in waxing. I gave her the lowdown.

"It's pretty straight forward. I dust a little powder on you, put a thin coat of wax on and pull it off, taking the hair with it. Yes, it hurts, but it's a quick hurt that fades rather fast. If you want just a cleanup, you can keep the undies on and I can work around them. If you want the whole thing done or a little triangle or strip, you strip down. You can always start with a basic wax and get comfortable with that before heading into Brazilian territory."

"Oh, Christine, I'm getting terrified just thinking about it."

"It hurts, but the pain is very short-lived, most people do fine, you can take a Tylenol or Ibuprofen before you come in."

"It's not the pain. I just don't think I could ever take my clothes off for you, I'd be *way* too embarrassed."

I reassured her like I do so many other women, "Nina, I do so many cha-cha waxes that the nudity doesn't even register with me anymore. It's really just another day at the office if that makes you feel any better."

"I'll think about it, I really want to try but I don't know if I can muster up the courage to do it."

"No pressure from me, but I would be happy to do it if you decide you want to go for it."

Nina continued her facials for the next few months and she'd tell me stories about getting back into the dating world, the men she was meeting, the perils and the pitfalls. She'd regale me with stories of disastrous dates, some of them funny, some of them kind of sad. It seemed as if she were meeting every bum, deviant, freeloader, criminal, sponger, and loser in the metro-area. She was a very kind person and after the garbage her ex had put her through, she deserved a good guy.

Nina also started to lose weight and get into shape, one of the side effects of divorce, I'm told. As a result, her physical confidence grew and she was talking about getting waxed again. She had started seeing a new guy and she thought waxing might be a nice surprise and a way to show her adventurous side. As her confidence grew, she was getting bolder in general and it looked good on her.

At her next facial, Nina expressed reluctance but she made a Brazilian appointment for a week later. She came in for her wax and as I was prepping, she said the same sort of thing that I hear from so many women, "Oh Christine, I'm *soooo* hairy. Don't be shocked. Don't look at my stomach. Oh, it's so gross. Sorry I didn't shave my legs. Oh, I need a pedicure. Don't look at my toes. They look so bad, I'm sorry."

Look, as long as your *business* is clean and your feet don't stink, you're good in my book. I don't even care if your feet are dirty, this is the land of flip flops and I've gotten used to the dirty black soles and it's not like hairy legs get in the way of a bikini wax anyway. If they are really furry, I might try to upsell you on a leg wax but that's about it.

"Babe, we are not going to be making out so if your legs are furry or your toes straggly, no worries."

Nina edged herself onto the table and she squirmed with embarrassment. She groaned and grimaced, her hands alternately covering her cha-cha and her face and I had not even started. I asked her what I ask most new clients, "Are we leaving anything behind?"

"Well, what are my choices?"

"Most people opt for everything off, some people like a strip of hair, some people like a petite triangle, some people like the thumb-size patch, I hate this one because it makes your vag look like it has a Hitler moustache, but technically the Brazilian is everything south of the Equator and whatever you want on the top."

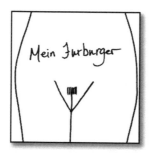

"The Equator?" she said confused.

"Yeah, you know, the Equator...uh, your clit."

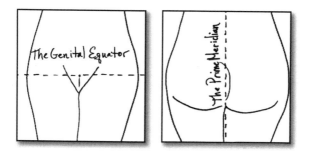

How's that for a geography lesson?

"Well what do *you* think?"

"I think you need to make your house pretty if you want some-one to come over, but this is not about what I want, what do *you* want?"

"I don't know what I want," she said, getting frustrated with all the options. "What do you have?"

"Okay. I have gone back and forth. I almost always go fully bare but sometimes when I want some contouring or to change it up a bit, I sport the petite triangle."

"Okay, give me what you've got."

Ripped

So I took it all off, and once she got over her embarrassment, she did better than I thought. Until she looked down.

"Christine, where did it all go, you *mugged* me. I got nothing left." She looked panicked.

"I thought you wanted it all off. You said 'give me what you've got'. I gave you what I've got," I said defensively.

"I meant the triangle, not everything. For Christ's sake, I look like a six-year-old."

"Oh Nina, I'm sorry, I totally misunderstood you."

"It's so *bald*." She said looking at her perfectly smooth skin.

"I am so sorry I misunderstood. I wish I had given you what you wanted. But, on the bright side," I reasoned with her, "unlike a bad haircut, not many people will see this as it grows out."

"Well, it's ok, I guess," she said as she continued to inspect herself. "It *is* really smooth. I'm just afraid that the boyfriend is going to think it's too much."

"Too much what?" I asked.

"Too much, you know, too much *vagina*."

"Nina, if my experience counts for anything, he will love it," I tried to reassure her.

"But why do they like it anyhow, is it because you look like a child cause that's *weird*."

"No, it's because men are visual creatures and with hair there, they can't see much. When you wax all the hair off, they get to see your bits and bobs. They also like the idea that you go through this complicated and painful ritual to present yourself to them. It's like you put your pussy on a silver platter."

She laughed and I took it as a good sign. "I don't know," she sighed, "but I guess we'll see. It's not like it's gonna grow back by tonight, right?"

She left and I beat myself up a little over the mistake. I didn't want to give her another reason to feel uncomfortable about her body. At the end of the day I knew it wasn't *that* big of deal, but I like clients to leave with what they wanted. I worked through the rest of the day, cleaned up, locked up and went home.

I returned to the spa the next day. I was the first one in and I turned all the lights on, got the wax warmers on and went to check the messages. The first one was from Nina, the time stamp on it was for somewhere around one in the morning. I got a panicky feeling that maybe she'd left okay but had become more upset about it and was going to give me a tongue lashing or worse. I held a cringe and listened for bad news.

Beep: (in a hushed voice) Hi Christine it's Nina. Oh my god! He absolutely lost his shit, I mean lost, his, shit. He went nuts, he spent like an hour just staring at it and the next hour with his face buried in it. We are so doing this from now on. Thank you, thank you, once again thank you, a thousand thank yous. Mark me down for the year.

I exhaled in relief. She was happy. I was happy.

ELEVEN

....

MY MOBY DICK

The first thing I hear from many of my new clients is how hairy they think they are. It's par for the course that a woman thinks something about her body is unusually and frighteningly disgusting. I reassure them that nope, you Madame, are no Yeti, and I *know* Yeti. Of course, some women are hairier than others, but generally even the hairiest woman is usually far less hairy than a near hairless guy. Women will come in for a Brazilian wax apologizing for a little leg hair as if a dense forest of gam growth could impede me from getting to their cha-cha. "We're not going to make out," I tease them, pretending to try to push through an imaginary forest of leg hair. "No reason to fret over a little stubble." Once in a while a client will require a trim before I can wax them. I hate trimming someone's pubic hair, but not for the reasons you might think. It's not because it makes me feel like I run a Supercuts for boush, or that I have to, you know, put my hands all over someone's pubic hair. Honestly, I am so used to pubic hair at this point. The only reason trimming creates a problem at all is because no matter how neat I try to be, little snipped pubic hairs fly everywhere. I then have one hell of a time figuring out which hairs are strays and which are attached. I go to do a final tweeze of any remaining hairs and the little snipped pubes are confusing and they seem to stick. I will try to brush them away with a towel to no avail. The only good way to remove them is blow them off, but I don't think there is a delicate way to blow the pubes off of someone's crotch. I bet if there *were* a polite way to do this, Martha Stewart would know. I think I just came up with her next segment. You are very welcome, Martha. And no matter how neat I am in clipping the hairs and putting them straight into the trash, I almost always find some later, usually when I am sitting down to eat lunch and realize it's on my arm or stuck in my bra. A little trim I can do, and super hairy clients are rarely a problem. Usually it's just people with some hair that they want gone. But every once in a while someone walks through the doors that could make even the most seasoned waxer cringe and break a sweat in anticipation of the work ahead.

My Moby Dick was Bridget, a Scotch-Irish girl with the most beautiful pale white skin and the coarsest black facial and body hair. Bridget not only had black hair against very white skin, but every closely-spaced follicle of hers had at least three, thick hairs shooting out of it. She had leg hair so dark and dense that even if she had just shaved, the black dots of the hair under the skin made her bare legs look gray with immediate 5 o'clock shadow and even just one day's growth would tear up your hand if you ran it up her leg. Bridget had the capability to grow a beard to rival any nineteen-year-old man and whereas most women sprout a little butt hair, her entire butt was hirsute. She was understandably self-conscious about being the poster child for excessive female hair growth. Bridget sought the refuge of waxing for several reasons. For one, shaving offered her nothing in the way of actual smoothness, her hair was so coarse that even the closest shave left stubble. Second, as mentioned, even if she shaved, she still sported the ever-present shadow. Third, shaving gave her, as it does many people, stubborn ingrown hairs. There's nothing like inflamed, weeping red cysts to add to the already painful self-consciousness of a very hairy girl.

As an esthetician and a strident feminist, I often struggle with my role in perpetuating the female beauty myth and upholding the Baseline Acceptable Rigid Female Standard of beauty. The Baseline Acceptable Rigid Female Standard of beauty or *BARFS,* definitely hurts women. Am I part of the problem? Am I helping people do something they already wanted to do or am I reinforcing the BARFS standard —a major tenet of which is the idea that women should be hairless, except the lush shiny stuff on their head and long doe-like lashes. Bridget with her hairy dilemma saw me as a savior of sorts and it felt good to know that I could help her. Sure, it's not like I was a doctor and Bridget was a third-world kid with a cleft palate, but still, my trade skills could help her feel better about herself and keep her out of the circus.

Bridget first came to me for an eyebrow wax. Then she added an upper lip wax and then we started waxing her chin regularly. With some weekend man plans coming up, Bridget wanted to be waxed from the waist down. I knew it would be time consuming and difficult, but she was game and I was willing to help. When someone has coarse and profuse growth, it is definitely more work for the esthetician, but it is also significantly more uncomfortable for the client. A thicker hair being pulled from the follicle hurts much more than a fine hair, just like a thicker needle hurts more going in than a fine one. Bridget had had several very large tattoos done, so I wasn't overly concerned about her pain threshold.

Bridget got naked save for a cotton wrap gown I gave her so she had a little coverage in between waxing different areas. She got on my table and I began with her leg wax. I dusted powder on the front of her legs; I smoothed a thin layer of wax over them; I pressed the fabric swath into the wax and pulled. Bridget's leg kicked into the air, reflexively. She groaned and her face twisted into a cartoon-like grimace. I think it is entirely possible that the model for Edvard Munch's *The Scream* came from a person experiencing their first body wax. I gave her a moment to recover from the shock of the pain. She took a deep, shaky breath and resettled herself on the table.

"The first one is the worst," I tried to reassure her. "Pretty soon your natural endorphins will kick in and temper the pain a bit."

I spread wax onto another section of skin, smoothed it down, and pulled.

"Jesus Christ," she exclaimed and again, her leg recoiled from me.

"Are you okay?" I asked.

"Yes, I'm fine. Keep going. It'll be worth it, it just hurts."

So I did a few more sections and every time, she winced in pain. Although she tried to be brave, her gasps, grunts, and watery eyes betrayed her stoic face. It was my first glimpse at what childbirth looked like.

After a *very* long twenty minutes, I finished the front of her legs and thighs.

"Flip over please."

As she did, I saw that the thick paper sheet that covered the table had practically dissolved from the profuseness of her butt sweat. It didn't matter that she knew I was friend not foe; her brain was telling her body I was the equivalent of a T. rex, creating the puddle of nervous flop sweat beneath her.

"Here," I offered, "let me put a new piece of paper down for you."

I removed the damp shreds of paper, soaked with the perspiration of fear. She lay face down on the crisp new paper sheet. As I started to work on the back of her legs, I saw that her hands were blanched from clenching.

I spread a thin layer of wax over the back of her calf, smoothed a piece of muslin over it and pulled. Where I waxed, small rivulets of blood seeped from each follicle. I dabbed her leg with a piece of tissue and kept at it. I finished her lower legs, and waxed her thighs before moving on to her bum. She had hair that grew horizontally across the cheeks of her bum and while most women require just a crack wax, I had to wax every inch of her posterior. The one good thing about a bum wax is that it is significantly less uncomfortable than the cha wax, or even the leg wax. I waxed strip after strip until her rear transformed from a hairy man-like one to a hairless lady butt. As I continued to work, her butt morphed in color from lily white to a deep, angry pink.

"Hang in there," I told her as I finished up her backside.

I asked her to flip over one more time, so that I could finish the service with her Brazilian wax. The paper sheet was again decimated from sweat, now streaked with blood from her poor, angry follicles. I put another new sheet on and had her lay down face up. I figured by now her endorphins would be pumping full blast perhaps providing some much needed pain relief. I bent her leg to the side and waxed one side of her cha. She had already trimmed for me but her hair was so dense that I had a hard time getting the wax enough contact it needed with the skin to pull the hair out. If the wax is on the hair but not on the skin, all you are doing is tugging a big clump of hair-- very hard, super painful and not effective for hair removal. So I decided to switch to my hard wax which works better in certain situations. It did, but between her sweating and bleeding, it was messy and a slow go. Her thick hairs we so resistant to coming out that I had to go over areas more than once and even when I went to tweeze some of the remaining stragglers, the hair wouldn't just slide out as it did with most clients. With Bridget, it was like there was someone on the other side pulling back. I had to put some real muscle into it and I'm pretty sure her thick, coarse hair broke my best tweezers.

The poor thing. She had so much thick hair that no matter how adept I was, or how gentle I tried to be, there was no way to make it even remotely comfortable. It was one of the first times in my career as a waxer where I really felt as if I were actually torturing someone. I finished up as kindly and quickly as I could. Her calves were flanked with dried blood speckles and her skin was red and swollen from the trauma, but after a few more minutes of tweezing, touch-ups, and a wipe off with a warm towel, she was hair free.

"You're finished." I told her apologetically and she looked at me like I had just unshackled her.

She stood up and as I held out the hand mirror in her direction and she perceptibly flinched.

"Oh my god, this is so much better," she stood admiring her smooth cha-cha and pale, hairless legs. She ran her hand up her smooth leg. "*Ahhh*," she purred, "No stubble and no shadow. I can wear a skirt. Chris, you are a miracle worker."

As we settled up I could see the exhaustion in her face. Lots of wussy clients complain about the pain, but clients like Bridget are entirely justified. I wasn't sure she'd be back and given the considerable level of pain she had had to endure, I didn't want to put any pressure on her. Truthfully, I think a part of me hoped that she wouldn't come in again because I hated to put someone through that, even when they wanted me to. It had also taken much longer than usual, but I felt uncomfortable charging her more because she had the bad luck to get the furry gene. It just seemed like a double slap in her hairy face to charge her more.

A few weeks later she called the spa. "I loved it Chris, it was awesome, and I wore short skirts for like two weeks before it started growing."

I was dismayed because for most people, waxing lasts from about four to six weeks. She went through all that pain to get a lousy two-week reprieve.

"I want to come in again but I am dreading the discomfort. Is there anything, anything I can do to make it less painful?"

"Well, you could definitely take a few over-the-counter pain relievers or pop something a little stronger if you have it."

"Well, I have some painkillers left over from my wisdom teeth."

"That would work but you should get a ride here if you are going to take the good stuff."

"I only live a few blocks away so I can just walk over. Anything else I can do?"

"Well, a bunch of places sell topical numbing agents. It won't eliminate the pain because it only numbs the surface. But again, it will at least reduce the discomfort."

"Okay, I'll get some of that."

She came in a week later armed with prescription pain relief and a topical numbing gel. The wax went better but truthfully, not much. Between the anticipated pain and the actual pain, Bridget was still terribly uncomfortable. I felt like Amnesty International might be at my doorstep any moment for the cruel and unusual punishment I was inflicting on the poor girl.

"Chris I absolutely love the results but I don't know if I can keep doing this. I know you are good and it's not your fault that it hurts so much, but this is torture for me."

"I know. You know, Bridget, you might want to think about laser hair removal. With light skin and dark hair, you are a very good candidate. It wouldn't rid you of *all* your hair but it would target the coarsest, darkest hair and even just a few sessions would thin out your hair and probably make the waxing more comfortable and you could do it less often."

"I would love to try laser but I just can't afford it."

"I wish I had a scholarship fund for laser hair removal treatments for women really in need."

"I know, isn't there like some Doctors Without Borders program for us hairy girls?"

"Sadly no, I think they are busy fixing cleft palates and zip lining."

Ripped

Bridget came in for her next appointment–the last in my day–armed with a small grocery bag and a plan. My assistant had left for the day so it was just the two of us.

"Ok, so, uh, I have an idea."

"Sure what?"

She set a sack on my reception desk and took out two tapered clear bottles. I turned to see the labels and rolled my eyes at her.

"You don't want me drinking here, is that it?"

"No, but really? *Zima*? Blech. I didn't think they even made Zima anymore."

"It's not like I can blend up a batch of margaritas and I can't pound beer, too burpy. It was either this or Boone's Farm."

"Yeah, sure. Pound some drinks. That might help."

"And this," she said, pulling out a little plastic baggy out of her jacket pocket. I looked closer and saw one expertly rolled joint.

"You can't smoke weed in here," I shook my head. "There is not enough lavender oil to get that smell out. If I don't let the staff microwave their lunch in the shop, I certainly can't let you go all Pineapple Express in the facial room. "

"Not in *here*. I thought maybe I could go around the back where the hair dressers are always smoking."

My spa was in one side of a converted duplex shared with an independently run hair salon on the other. "Sure, the owner just got back from a two month crack bender so I'm pretty sure she won't blink an eye if she sees you smoking a little weed."

We stepped outside and made ourselves at home on the rusted patio table by the salon side and Bridget lit up. After several long pulls from the joint, she held it in my direction while swilling down the other half of her first Zima.

"I think it's wise if one of us is sober, no?" I replied. "You know, if you are going to have a bar tab and a drug trade every time you wax, getting laser might end up being the more affordable of the two."

"Hah, a guy at this party gave me the joint. It might just be schwag, who knows. You're probably right but I've looked into it and I have so much, so much…" she paused looking for the right words, "so much *surface* area that needs hair removal that with multiple sessions, we're talking about thousands of dollars and it's *still* not guaranteed to get rid of all the hair. Maybe if I got a better job at some point. My job sucks. I fucking hate it. The pay is bad and I just don't have that kind of money and I'm not sure I'd even do it if I did. Which I don't. It doesn't matter because we are going to do this and it's gonna be great because I am feeling *pretty* good and you are really good at this Chris and I really like you and am I acting weird? Cause I feel kind of weird. "

Clearly the marijuana was the real deal.

Bridget finished up and we went back to the treatment room.

"You know the drill," I told her and she stepped into the changing room to undress, leaving the curtain open while she pulled off her pants. She got caught up in her pant leg and almost fell over.

"Goddamfuckinpants. You know I met this guy last weekend, Bob, and I'm serious, Bob is so gonna get fucked this weekend, because I'm going to be all pretty and shit and he's not going to be able to *stand* it." I was beginning to see another side of Bridget and stoned Bridget had kind of a potty mouth. She stood naked looking at me a little unsure.

"Here, put this on," I said as I picked up the wrap gown and held it toward her. She put it on and climbed onto the table face up. Again, I started with the front of her legs. The hair still roughly tugged its way out of the follicles and they still bled with the trauma, but Bridget seemed much more comfortable.

"How was that?" I asked.

"Okay, actually not so bad."

I continued with the front of her legs, finishing them up, as Bridget talked nonstop. I looked at her to see how she was doing and she was staring at me.

"You know Chris, you are really pretty. I mean, I've always thought you were pretty, but now that I'm like, like really *looking* at your face, really *looking*, you're so beautiful. Like if Michelle Williams and Drew Barrymore had a baby, she'd look just like you. That's how fucking gorgeous you are."

Now I don't care who you are, being told how *fucking* gorgeous you are, no matter how totally high the other person is, feels good. This wax was going measurably better for both of us.

"Turn over so I can do the back of your legs and your bum," I told her. She flopped over onto her stomach. I finished her legs and moved on to the bikini wax. I did the first strip and she grabbed my wrist with her hand.

"Stop!" She said seriously.

"What's the matter?" I asked, thinking I had hurt her or her superhero buzz was wearing off.

"Do you have any food here?"

"Honey this isn't In & Out," I said both relieved that I hadn't hurt her and annoyed that she was dragging this on with her early-onset munchies.

"No seriously, you have to have a granola bar or something, I am so fucking hungry."

"You're going to have to wait. We're almost done."

"Can I just go grab something and come back?"

"No you *cannot*."

"But I'm *sooooo* hungry, this is really *serious*," she said with a completely straight face. "I would give you fifty dollars for some Cheetos." Being financially motivated, I considered running to the convenience store on the corner but it was getting late and I just wanted to get home. Plus, I would like to think I might feel bad about taking hunger money from a stoned woman just trying to get through a bikini wax.

"Seriously, I think you can wait another twenty minutes and then buy yourself some Cheetos on the way home."

"I'm sorry, I'll stop. I'm fine. I can wait, I guess." She paused, "No, I don't think I can. Oh god, I'm so hungry. Make it stop!"

"Listen, if I find you something, will you knock it off and be still so we can finish?" I said feeling positively parental.

"Yes," she said, looking cautiously optimistic.

I came back a few minutes later. "Here, I found some wasabi peas and a bag of Cheese Nips. It's all I have and they are probably stale as they were hiding at the bottom of my filing cabinet." Bridget grabbed the bags out of my hand before I could finish.

While Bridget ate, I finished up the wax. "How are you feeling?" I asked.

"Fine. I'm a little tired but that wasn't so bad." She got up to get dressed and I brought her a bottle of water.

"Here, drink this," I told her. We went to the front and settled up. I looked her over and she looked ready to crash. Between the booze, the weed, and the high-gear endorphin rush of waxing, she was coming down quick.

"Ok Chris, I will see you soon. Thanks." She got up and shuffled toward the door. The idea of her walking home, even just a few blocks, seemed like a really bad idea at this point.

"Bridget, let me take you home."

"No, I'll be fine. It's not far."

"No, I really think it's better if I take you home. All freshly waxed, too much walking is bound to irritate everything and we don't want to disappoint Bob, right?"

She looked at me, "Haaa, no we don't."

"Well, then come on, let's go."

The next morning I came in to get set up for a busy day. I cleared the Zima bottles from the front and the circle of Cheez-It crumbs from around the bed. It felt kind of like cleaning up a party you had not been invited to. This kind of party every few weeks might be more than I could take.

A few weeks later I was having lunch with a friend of mine who had recently taken a job with an esthetic clinic that did Botox, laser facials, and hair removal when she mentioned that they were looking for a new receptionist. In addition to a relatively generous salary and benefits package, the doctor who owned the practice offered accrued free services for employees, including hair removal. A phone call to Bridget armed with a personal referral and she was well on her way to a great new job and free hair removal. Sure, I was down a client, but I had performed a mitzvah of sorts, and after all the torture I had inflicted on the women of Southern California, my karma probably needed it.

TWELVE

....

HONEY DON'T EAT THE HAIRY GUM

Have you ever thought about how you would commit the perfect murder? No? Oh, then me neither. I used to think that the perfect murder would be taking your intended victim on a boat, getting them a little drunk and then getting that vessel going at top speed and just chucking your persona non grata right off the boat à la Natalie Wood. You could also put a little sleepy-time pill in their drink so they don't fight back too hard or even hit them with a rock and throw the rock overboard with them. That way, some forensic savant would match up the rock pattern with their head trauma and it will look like they hit the rock rather than the rock hit *them*. Just make sure it is a rock that is from the same area and not some rock that will draw attention to itself. The more I think about it, if the cops found the rock, it would probably not have the barnacles and seaweed growing on it that the other mid-ocean bottom rocks would. That might be a tip off. Better if you go diving a few weeks before, find a good rock in the same area and use *that* rock so it will blend with the other rocks. But don't let anyone witness you pulling up big, barnacaly rocks. That might arouse suspicion. Ok, the rock is a bad idea–way too complicated, don't do that.

The alternate plan would be to lure your victim to the local high-volume waxing establishment. You could pick from any of the garden-variety methods once you are there. Get creative, really make your mark. Just make sure there are no witnesses putting you and your victim together and make sure you get rid of the weapon. Other than that, you are in the clear. The amount of physical evidence at the crime scene would be *overwhelming*. Think about it, tens of thousands of hairs floating around the room, more skin cells then you can imagine. Random bits of DNA everywhere you look. And I don't even want to think about what the place would look like under a black light. It would probably take the CSI guys years just to *process* all of the DNA evidence, much less find a match. I think on the remote chance you were charged, even some young, fresh-out-of-night-school lawyer could make a case for reasonable doubt.

"Well your honor, just because my client's pubic hair was found at the scene doesn't mean anything, given that five-hundred-seventy other pubic hairs have been identified from the same location."

I think that I have more than adequately proven my case, and that I am watching way more Forensic Files than is healthy.

One of the downsides to the work of waxing is that it can be kind of messy. I am a tidy person and I keep my spa very clean, but wax is wax. It is sticky, tacky, drippy, gooey, and steadfast. As a seasoned waxer, I have become more and more careful to not make a mess. Still, no matter how neatly I try to work, wax is not easily removed once it has adhered itself to things. I constantly pick wax off of my nails. I pull threadlike filaments of wax from my face, hair, and clothes. I sit at home after a long day of waxing and wordlessly note the pubic hairs affixed with wax to the bottom of my shoes while I eat dinner with my family. I am forever cleaning wax off of something. It is like a territorial war where the wax tries to advance its position as I try to hold it back with vigilance, keeping its stronghold small and contained. There is wax dripped on the floor that requires solvent, a wooden spatula and a strong arm before it relents. There is wax on the wall where I threw a wax-covered spatula in the trash but missed and it stuck to the wall instead. There are thin wax threads that are like spider webs that start to cover the table holding the wax.

In the work of keeping the wax from taking over, I have sometimes carried it too far. For instance, I spent my first few years scraping wax off of a two-dollar trash can before it hit me that I'm spending time scraping wax off of a two-dollar trash can. Maybe it was the cheap Midwesterner in me or the planet hugger, but eventually I came to the conclusion that all the solvent I had to use to revive the waxy trash can was likely as bad for the environment as just getting a new one. Now I have a stash of two-dollar pristine white plastic trash cans ready to step into battle when the current one is getting too grungy. One piece of advice I will give to spa and salon owners is to keep your place clean. And for goodness sake, if things look worn, replace them. You run a business not a depression-era tenement apartment complex. If your towels get ragged, use them to clean, not on a client. If your massage sheets smell like salad dressing even after a good hot water washing, for God's sake, just throw them out. No client should have to look at an oily stain on a sheet and hope they have been laundered. Perception is reality and if you take shortcuts on clean, your business will suffer. Stylists too are guilty of the dirties. Let me tell you, when you are sitting getting your hair shampooed, that glob of conditioner on the armrest will make you think of sperm every single time. Sure you *know* it's conditioner but the first thing your brain will go to is sperm. My spa has always been clean and well maintained. Yet I have never been able to get the floors truly clean. I sweep, mop, and scrub but with old, cracked wooden floors and waxy residue, they may *look* clean but don't examine them too closely. The floors get a regular once over, but thankfully the old pitted, weathered wood hides a lot of the grunge. At the spa, the oft-used five-second rule with regard to dropped food should never apply. Even a dropped hard-shelled M&M goes straight into the bin never to be seen again.

A few years ago, a regular of mine brought her daughter with her to her wax appointment. I normally do not let kids in the spa because they are gross and I hate them. Kids mess with the water cooler, walk into occupied massage rooms, open up two-hundred-dollar face creams and stick their fingers in it and then their moms hand it to me like I have a magic wand to make it sellable again. Kids roll around on their Heelys on my wooden floors, making dents in the fifty plus year old wood while their moms count out a three-dollar tip on a seventy-five-dollar service. The reality is, if you are bringing your kids to a spa, you probably don't get it. But in the case of this client, I let her seven-year-old daughter in the room with us. Her babysitter had cancelled last minute, her anniversary was coming up, and she didn't want to reschedule. She was my last client of the day and my assistant had already gone home, so I didn't want to leave the kid up front alone to manhandle my water cooler or worse. There was a chair in a far corner of the room and I told the little girl she could sit down. Her mom didn't seem to be bothered by the thought of her daughter witnessing her getting hair ripped from her genitals, but it bothered me. It's bad enough that we women have so much weirdness and shame attached to normal body stuff, the thought of being introduced to the idea of waxing at such a young age was a little disturbing.

Of course like any seven-year-old worth her salt, the girl would not stay on the fucking chair for more than two minutes at a time. She wanted to see what I was doing and really, I didn't think she needed to see inside her mother's cavernous vagina while I waxed her butthole. Her mom was useless, so I had to keep shoulder checking the nosy parker. She was undeterred. I told her to go wash her hands at the sink just to keep her busy. That depleted an almost new glass bottle of French orange-blossom hand soap in no more than three minutes. Then she started pressing the buttons on a four-thousand-dollar microdermabrasion machine.

"Honey, don't touch that," I said. Then she started scooting all over the floor like a dog with a dingleberry. It was gross but at least she was out of my hair, never mind she was elbow deep in everyone else's. I certainly wouldn't let my own kids crawl around the filthy floor, but it served her right. Yep, stick those fingers right in your mouth, you disgusting moppet.

While on her hands and knees exploring the DNA soup that is my floor, she apparently hit the jackpot.

"Mom I found some gum can I have it?" And here is where never saying no to your kids gets totally awesome. The mom says yes and as my brain starts calculating why there would be a perfectly good, wrapped piece of gum somewhere on my floor it hits me. Before I can stop her, it was already in her mouth.

"Mom I think this gum is hairy," she said, chewing no less vigorously.

"Oh honey, don't eat the hairy gum. Oh no, spit that out." Her mom said and didn't even sit up just shot her arm around and cupped it in front of her daughter's mouth. I held the trash can out for her and apologized even though it was not at all my fault that she told her daughter she could eat something off of my floor.

"It's okay, she eats her boogers. Didn't seem to bother her," said Mom. This is what happens when, three kids in, you just stop worrying about the little things, like your kids chewing wax laced with strangers' pubes.

THIRTEEN

···

BACK, SAC & CRACK: THE BAD BOYS OF WAXING

"I booked you a new sac wax, his name is Jerry and he's coming in at eleven," my assistant Brooke informed me.

"Great, how did he sound?" I asked, as always assuming that if some guy is a pervy creep, he will no doubt have the pervy creep phone voice to go with it.

"I dunno. He just sounded like a dude who wants his junk waxed."

"Fair enough. When he gets here, have him fill out the new client form."

I am notoriously lazy and forgetful about new client forms. When I first started I was maniacal about this because it was how I sent out postcards and promos. Now that I'm consistently busy, it's spotty at best. But I always, always, make new *male* waxing clients fill it out. It is the first prong in my three-prong approach to making certain my male clients are fully aware that this is a professional service and not a tug job. Making clients write their name and address and other personal information that I have about them and they don't have about me draws an imaginary line between us. I think of it as my thin pink line.

Ripped

The second prong in my anti-happy-ending campaign is my lab coat. I rarely wear my lab coat, but when it's a manzilian, at least a new one, I wear that coat like it's armor. It lends a clinical air to things that again, sends the message to the client, I am like their *doctor* so please no grab ass, mister. Now, yes, I am aware that wearing the white lab coat while I tear hair from the genitals might actually *heighten* the fantasy for some men. That's why I don't wear a nurse cap and stilettos with bobby socks with it. For most men, the lab coat nips any insidious ideas in the bud.

The third prong in my *prongless* waxing service is what I refer to as the *dignity towel*. The dignity towel is what covers the penis through most of the service. Sure I move the dignity towel around, and yes, I see every part of the penis, testicles and butt at some point during the service. And yes, I am touching penises but it's through a towel so it doesn't count. Sure, the dignity towel is about as effective as a backless hospital gown, but it allows male clients to retain some dignity while protecting my eyeballs at least a little.

A man has a penis and I *don't* have a penis, so no matter how many *manzilians* I *manscape*, it has never become routine and humdrum the way it has with female clients. While returning male clients still make me a tad anxious, new male clients are really hard. Maybe 'really hard' is not the best wording, except sometimes they are.

I started the day in question as I do most, although I was a bit nervous. As I finished up a brow wax, Brooke popped her head in the open door of my waxing room. "You're next client Jerry is here."

"Thank you. Is he up front?" I asked.

"Yeah, he's finishing filling out the new client form."

"Great. Please tell him I'll be up in a few minutes."

I finished up my client and walked her to the front to check out and book her next appointment. I passed by the couches where I saw the child of a woman getting her hair colored, a soccer mom on her cell phone and an old guy reading a newspaper. We have a big beauty supply adjacent to the salon and I figured my client had wandered off to check out the hair paste and guy grooming gunk that the twenty-somethings are so fond of. I went back to my room and checked that it was prepared for a Brazilian and walked back to our front reception area to find Jerry.

"Hey, do you know where my client is?" I asked Brook.

"Yeah, he's on the couch," she said.

"No, he's not there anymore, I looked. I thought maybe he came over here to look at hair stuff."

Brooke craned her head around the corner, looking into reception.

"No, he's right there. That's Jerry," she said motioning with her head at the couch where the old man sat.

I looked at the couch with the old man, "No, that's not him." I said dismissively, shaking my head.

"Oh, *yes* it is," my assistant said with wide eyes and a big grin.

It's not that I was skeeved out that the guy was in his sixties. I was just totally taken aback because most of the guys coming in for a wax are in their twenties or thirties, well-groomed, and in good shape. This guy was probably in his late sixties with gray balding hair, a sizable potbelly, and what looked like mild arthritis. I switched into slightly out-of-body autopilot, which is what I do when I am in an uncomfortable situation. Part of my discomfort was the fact that since this guy didn't fit the usual demographic, I wondered if this was a sign he was going to be creepy or do something weird or at the very least be completely unprepared for the nudity and pain involved.

"Hi Jerry, I'm Chris," I said with a big fake Miss-America smile plastered to my face. "You can come on back with me." Jerry followed me back without a word. "So you are here for a Brazilian wax?" I asked, thinking maybe there had been some confusion about the service itself.

"Yes." Jerry said nodding his head.

"Which is *everything*," I said, as I used my palm to pantomime a circle over my own lower half just to be sure Jerry understood the area I was talking about.

"Yep."

I stepped out to let Jerry undress, giving him my usual spiel about naked from the waist down, face up, dignity towel over your, uh, yourself. I knocked a few minutes later.

"Uh, hold on," Jerry said. I heard some groans and grunts and imagined Jerry in there furtively jacking off all over my treatment room, apparently the idea of me just too much for him. I knocked again and held my breath.

"Ok, I'm ready." I opened the door, afraid of what I might find. Would Jerry's seed be dripping from my pretty sage green walls or was Jerry waiting to finish in my direction as soon as I opened the door? As usual, life is much more colorful, graphic, and disturbing in my imagination because Jerry just lay on the treatment bed stiffly, looking both physically and emotionally uncomfortable.

"Sorry, with my arthritis it was a little tough to get up here." I smiled and took a deep breath and assessed the work before me.

Jerry was not my run-of-the-mill client. So many of my male clients who seek deforestation are very focused on how they look. They often want a smooth groin to go with flat abs and tanned skin. Jerry, on the other hand, looked more like a lost roadie from some Grateful Dead touring bus than a follicle-phobic metrosexual. Jerry splayed out on my table naked from the waist down was a preview of what aging brings. It was a close up, non-airbrushed look at the body of a sixty something man. Jerry had old-man legs–veined and lumpy with gnarled joints and dry, ugly feet. He was not particularly hairy, which would make the work easier but with arthritis and what looked like gout, it might be harder to contort him into the positions that make waxing possible. On top of that, Jerry's rotund belly rested on the top part of his pubis obscuring part of the area I would need to get to, and a jagged, somewhat fresh scar was gouged into his lower abdomen. I inquired about the scar.

"From my gallbladder surgery. It's been a few months, but it's still a little sensitive." Jerry's legs were a bruised map of the circulatory system in a palette of blues, greys, and muddied flesh tones. His skin was dull and his mostly balding scalp was shiny in places. I began the service doing what I always do while I struggled to make small talk and stay composed.

"Chris, do you have a pillow or something I can put under my head? Laying flat like this my lower back keeps spasming." I grabbed a pillow and tried to help him get more comfortable.

Lucky for me, Jerry was pleasant enough. Sure, he reminded me of my grandpa a little but after a few minutes, it was bearably awkward. I struggled to find something to talk to him about. He was a retired teacher but he told me he still coached boy's basketball. I found he loved music so we usually talked about the Beatles and Fleetwood Mac, two likes we had in common.

Why did he come see me? Jerry had had prostate surgery. In prep for the surgery, a nurse had completely shaved him. He was indifferent, but his wife loved it and Jerry loved his wife. After months of shaving and fighting his failing vision and an unsteady arthritic hand, he decided to put himself in my hands, literally, and set his embarrassment aside to try waxing.

He was good through the wax and only cried a little. He added a nose and ear hair removal and all of it took me about forty-five minutes. His total came to just under a hundred bucks and he left me a crisp hundred and a twenty dollar bill. He turned out to be one of my most generous, consistent clients.

I came home that day and told my husband all about Jerry.

"That's kind of weird. I can't imagine someone that old caring too much about pubic hair."

"I know, right?" I said.

"How did it look?"

"How did what look?"

"You know, his penis."

"It's funny, it just looked like a penis. His body looked old and his skin had a lot of sun damage but his penis looked like any other penis. I guess they are kind of ageless really. Probably because it's never in the sun. That's why I use sunscreen so regularly, so I can have ageless skin, like Jerry's penis," I joked.

"I wonder if nudists have older looking penises because they're probably in the sun more. Yeah, I bet their penises look much older," he said matter-of-factly.

"Jerry's balls looked pretty old and wrinkled though," I added.

"My balls looked ninety the day I was born."

"You're right, balls just look kind of old and wrinkled from the get-go huh?"

Male clients are definitely a different ball game than my ladies. Erections? Yes, they happen. Think about it; a heterosexual man lying naked in front of an attractive woman who is meticulously eyeing their package as she first powders it, then oils the rest of it up, and then slathers it with warm wax. Yes, many, though not all men, sport a little wood at the beginning of the service. These pre-game erections never last very long because the second I start pulling the hair from their bodies, the turtle goes back in its shell.

I have had my share of odd clients. They get their self-explanatory nicknames like Hairpants and Poopypants, Mona the Moaner, Chia Puss, Elephant Ears, Teenwolf, Toots McGee, Yeti, and Superfly Afrotastic. It should be known, however, that most of my clients are perfectly normal men and women who just want less body and facial hair, fewer wrinkles, clearer pores, softer skin, well-groomed eyebrows, dark lashes, pretty hands and feet, and unkinked muscles. Still, when you work on enough people, some of them are going to fly their freak flags higher than others.

The first time David came to me, it was for a back wax. This wasn't remarkable in any way because guys get their backs waxed all the time. The back wax is probably the single most common male waxing service I do. It is also the easiest waxing service there is—just one flat expanse that can't be reached by the owner. I always finish this service with a warm towel and a quick but nice application of anti-itch lotion which usually leads to a nice tip. David was friendly and nice enough and made an appointment to come in again. The next time I saw him, he added a chest wax to his back wax. Again, this isn't uncommon because some guys start with a back wax and find they like it so much they want to try their chest too. He was a good client, arrived on time, didn't fuss too much, followed directions, and tipped well.

The third time David came in, he said he would like to try waxing his legs. Now very few guys wax their legs, almost none, but David told me he played water polo and he thought it might help his game. He praised waxing while I pulled the hair from his legs. He told me he had shaved before and appreciated the lack of stubble and ingrown hairs with waxing. He seemed so calm, so utterly relaxed, that I applauded his pain threshold. "You're a tough one," I said, "most guys do a whole lot more whining." David just lay there with this almost serene look on his face.

The next time he came in, he asked if I had time to add a Brazilian and maybe wax his underarms. Now this was a bit more unusual. It's not so uncommon that a guy will get his junk waxed, but underarms were a bit of a red flag. Still, who am I to say what should be hairy or not. So I set out to do the job. It was when I went to go wax his junk that I realized he had an erection. The erections themselves are not such a big deal, they normally go away after the pain of waxing begins. Dave's erection however, had snuck up after I started waxing. Through my underwhelming powers of observation, I noticed that the pain of waxing itself appeared to be the cause of the arousal. David was my first masochist.

I completed the service slightly skeeved out, but he wasn't touching himself or me so I felt no boundaries had been crossed. Only afterward did I sit down and think, should I find this upsetting? Is this weirder than it seems? That night, I had dinner with Lana, another esthetician I know. Lana was a goth-punk beauty who had seen corners of the world I had not, so I thought she might be better equipped to understand this. I filled her in on the day.

"Is it weird that he was clearly enjoying the service?" I asked.

"Did he get off?

"No, I don't think so," I said a little unsure.

"You remember when I was having money problems and Barb tried to hook me up with that guy that wanted some girl to come and beat the shit out of him?"

"Ick, yes I remember."

"Well, he was prepared to pay me like fifteen-hundred dollars for an hour of torture, so if you ask me, if your client was in it for the beating, he got off cheap."

"Are you saying I should charge him more or stop seeing him?" I asked.

"Unless it's making you uncomfortable or he tries to jack off in the room, I say just up your fee. Either he will go away or at least you'll be raking in enough cash to make the weirdness worth it. With the market's steep price tag for a good beating, if you ask me, you should definitely be charging more."

I did start charging him more and David kept coming in every few months. Though I never got used to him all blissed out while I waxed him, the money was hard to pass up. Still, when he stopped coming in, I was a little relieved. Apparently he had found someone who hurt him better than I did and in this instance, I was happy to be second best.

Trisha, an esthetician I worked with chatted with me over lunch on the issue of male waxing clients.

"I just couldn't wax a guy," Trisha said shaking her head. "Truthfully, I don't even like waxing their backs, but definitely not their penis and stuff," she said cringing. Trisha preferred not to work with male clients at all. "Men have a very difficult time separating the sensual from the sexual. You rub a woman's shoulders, she is grateful, you rub a man's and he starts looking at you weird. Men don't quite understand the whole nurturing touch thing."

I, on the other hand, felt like to refuse male clients would be discriminatory. I considered it a matter of professionalism that I treated both male and female clients. It's not like a nurse refuses male patients. But Trisha had a point because men *do* see the services differently than women and the complications of male clients are infinitely more, well, *complicated.*

"A Brazilian is not exactly nurturing touch for men or women," I pointed out. "Man? Woman? It's not that different," I tried to convince her.

"Oh, *it's* different alright."

"Come on, the triangle part is essentially the same male or female, dude ass is certainly *uglier* but mechanically the same. The only real difference is the balls. Well, and the base of the penis. I do usually have to wax that and there's no real female equivalent to it."

"I couldn't do it. As for my husband, I'm pretty sure he wouldn't like me hanging out with someone else's penis."

"Gene doesn't care," I said matter-of-factly.

"How can he not care?"

"First, Gene knows his penis is the only one I even like. And with a job, three kids, two cats, two rats, a dog, some frogs and only twenty-four hours in the day, even *that* usually requires a margarita and a back rub first. Second, I am very clinical about the whole thing. If Gene felt like I saw it as the least bit sexual, yes, he would be weirded out. If I was like, oh baby, it was cock in the morning and cock in the evening, cock, cock, cock, *wheeee*, I *looooves* waxing cock..."

"*Stop,*" Trisha interrupted laughing. "I know you don't see it as sexual but what if *they* do?"

"I'm so detached. Maybe I'm able to wax guys because I've never had good boundaries. Besides, none of my male clients are inappropriate. If they were, I would be a lot more hesitant working on men, but they are just normal people who want hair removal, nothing more. I have never had a guy client be weird or make me feel uncomfortable."

I did it. I jinxed myself. I said the word *never* and I had made it so. I had gone years without incident. I'd had only regular guys who never creeped me out or asked me inappropriate questions or tried to touch me or made the service feel, somehow, *unsavory*. Sure I waxed an old guy's balls and a pain freak, but they were no big deal. Then I open my big mouth and I get two nutjobs (pun intended) in that very same week.

Mitch definitely made the naughty list. The first thing I noticed about him was that he was very short, like *hobbit* short. I stand just over five feet and we were nearly eye-to-eye. The second thing was that Mitch didn't look like most of the guys requesting Brazilian waxing. He wasn't a fit metrosexual, a gym rat, a newly divorced man with a twenty something girlfriend or a fuzzy twink. Still, while there are definitely 'types' with male Brazilian waxing clients, there are plenty of clients who don't fit them.

"Hi I'm Chris, the esthetician," I said reaching out to shake his hand.

"I'm Mitch." His hand limply circled my fingers rather than my hand and gave a half-hearted pump. I have had more confident handshakes from a golden retriever. Mitch briefly eyeballed my chest and I regretted wearing the dress I had on. The dress was a short-sleeve floral in a mix of white, blues, and greens. It was loose fitting, came to my knees and was cut well above any cleavage, but the thick t-shirt type material and elasticized, empire waist that fit snugly under my boobs made them look like large, fleshy torpedoes. I customarily dress more conservatively or wear my lab coat when I have a male Brazilian, especially a client I am unfamiliar with, but Mitch was added to the schedule that same day, it was in the middle of a very hot summer day and my lab coat was crumpled in the dirty towel's bag, waiting to be taken home and laundered.

"How did you come to find us, Mitch?" I asked, using the word *us* to somehow imply I had some backup.

"My girlfriend Ashley comes here."

Good, I thought, I prefer when male clients are referred to me by other clients.

"Which Ashley?" I asked trying to place which of my many Ashleys he was referring to. Since most women talk about their significant (and insignificant) others, if I could remember her, I could probably remember what she had told me about him.

"Well, she *used* to come here. She moved back north with her parents. She's my ex," he added.

"Ok," I said trying to think of an Ashley that moved up north with her parents, not ringing any bells.

"Follow me, I'll take you to the waxing area and give you the rundown on what you can expect." I held back on my usual funny banter because I already sensed this guy might misread friendly as flirty.

I stood in the doorway after leading Mitch into the treatment room. "The male Brazilian includes the top, the testicles and the bum, do you want everything taken off?" I asked.

"Yeah, everything."

"Okay, then you will remove your clothing from the waist down and sit here," I said motioning to the middle of the waxing table as I always do. "This is what we call the *dignity towel*." I held up the small, green hand towel. "You will use this towel to cover yourself up," I said as I motioned to the groin area, "and I will use it to move things around. It allows you a bit of modesty and allows me to focus on the area that I am waxing. There is a good deal of discomfort in your first wax but once it is over, the pain dissipates very quickly. I will start you just lying down, face up with your legs straight out and then I will have you pull your legs up to your chest when I wax your bum. Do you have any questions?"

"Nope."

"Then I will step out, give you a few minutes to undress and I will knock before I come in." I closed the door behind me and walked over to the front desk.

Ripped

"I really wish I had not been wearing this dress today," I told Jackie, one of our receptionists.

"Yeah, it makes your boobs look huge." She squinted and leveled her gaze on my chest, "Chris I think I can see your nipple." I looked down and because I had a nearly transparent bra on and the thin, patterned dress I wore just happened to have a big white blotch near my left breast, it did, in fact, expose a little rosy shadow of nipple.

"Fuck me."

"Here, just put a piece of paper towel in your bra." she said ripping off a piece from beside the coffeemaker. I shoved the scrap of paper towel under the transparent section. By the way, this shows why having a great assistant can be critical in any business. It isn't just anyone that will spot and MacGyver your visible nips.

"That's better. But your titties still look awesome–not good Chris, not good," Jackie said soberly, shaking her head like a disappointed head mistress.

I returned to the treatment room, knocked, and entered. Mitch lay on the bed naked from the waist down as requested, but his small, uncircumcised penis lay against his thigh. Well, it was not actually *touching* his thigh because it was notably small but rather, it leaned in the general direction of his thigh. I looked around for the towel I had given him to cover up. I saw a little corner of green poking out from under his leg. I grasped the corner of the towel and pulled it out from under him.

"Here, this is for you," I said flatly and put it over his penis. I didn't want to appear too bitchy because sometimes people are nervous and they don't understand my instructions. I have told women to get undressed from the waist down for a Brazilian and I come in and they are completely naked. I have asked little old ladies to fasten the facial gown around them like a bath towel only to come in and they are wearing it like a skirt with their boobs hanging untethered for all to see. Mitch would not be the first client to get it wrong. Maybe Mitch had just misunderstood my directions. Yet, it *felt* a little like I was being forced to look at his penis, head on, but I was going to assume it was accidental and not some kind of semi-sanctioned exhibitionism.

With the towel now covering his penis, I dusted some powder on the triangle-shaped top of his pubic hair. His rotund belly was resting on his pubic mound right in my way. "Put your hands like this," I said, placing his fat little palms on his fat little belly, "and pull toward you." He held his stomach and I slathered wax on him and then rip, rip, rip, the top was done.

"Doing ok?" I asked him.

"Yeah."

I threw the spatula and strip in the trash behind me and when I turned back to Mitch, the towel was laying against his thigh leaving his penis, now semi-erect, exposed yet again. His handshake might have been limp but his mini-Mitch was not.

Now this is probably the point where someone with better boundaries would put their stuff down, look the client square in the eye and say get dressed, we are done and you will pay me for the service. Me? My mind is still trying to process exactly what is going on and while it's busy doing that, I just keep going. Sometimes I don't know how I didn't end up in some stranger's car by the time I was ten.

I looked at Mitch, trying to read him, and he appeared nonplussed. I took the towel, put it back over his junk, and grabbed one of his stumpy hands and unceremoniously plunked it down on his woody and stretched it to the side making his scrotum skin taut. Was I going to need to get a paperweight out to keep that towel on him? With most clients, I use very small pieces of hard wax on the testicles to minimize discomfort and avoid tearing skin. With Mitch, in an effort to wrap this up, send him on his way, and maybe even curb the erection, I took off big swaths of testy hair. The erection didn't subside and now it was as if his penis was *mocking* me. I looked at Mitch again and he just returned my gaze, he was *unbending*. If this weren't a hostile erection, wouldn't he be at least a little embarrassed?

I held his eye contact with my own steely gaze while I moved his hands to the other side and pulled them so I could wax the rest of his sac. In my head, I gave Mitch a verbal dressing down in the style of Simon Cowell, "your penis is utterly forgettable, small in stature and rather amateurish. It is awful and I hate it. I almost mistook it for a child's thumb." This made me feel better in the moment, even though it was an imaginary revenge. I worked quickly on the other side.

"Now pull your legs up to your chest and I will wax your bum," I said. He seemed to have a little trouble mustering the stomach muscles to pull his legs up, so I pushed his knees towards his chest. Go easy, I told myself, this might be just what he needs to fill the old spank bank of his. Two cursory rips on either side of his ass and I told him he was done.

Whereas most clients get cleaned up, dewaxed and aloefied, Mitch and his stupid penis got no further touching from me. I threw a butt wipe toward him. "You can clean yourself up with this," I said as I left the room, hoping that wasn't an invitation for him to finish himself off in my pretty little spa room. I gave the girls his total and went to hide in the break room until he left, not wanting to have to fake any niceties.

When I was certain the coast was clear, I headed back to the front desk to pull his credit card slip.

"No tip–you have got to be fucking kidding me."

"Skunked you?"

"Yeah. The little fucker has a boner the whole time and then doesn't tip."

"Does that happen a lot?"

"No. Once in a while a guy will get a semi at the beginning but it goes away. This wasn't like that. It felt super creepy."

"Ew."

"Ew is right, *troll*. Add him to my No-Fly List," I told her.

Two days after Mitch and his tedious but persistent boner, I had a back and chest wax scheduled with Steven. Steven had been coming to me for waxing for a few months. He leered a little and always talked about his marriage problems, but was otherwise harmless.

The first time Steven came in was without incident. He wanted a back wax and a back wax he got. The only personal information he revealed was that he was trying to get back in shape and didn't want to be hairy at the gym. He was nice enough and told me I would see him in a couple of weeks to do it again. A month or two later, he came back in. Again, I waxed only his back. I told him he looked like he had dropped some weight. This might seem like an inviting comment but I always try to remember something my clients and I talked about so they know I listen to and remember them. It is one of the things that helps build relationships and I have a good memory that I like to show off.

Steven commented that he was really trying and thanked me for noticing. He then lamented that his wife hadn't seem to notice and she was the one who had put the pressure on him to get back into shape. I finished up the wax and he left.

Here's the thing–it is not at all unusual for clients to reveal personal things to me. It's the nature of two people in a room together with no one else to overhear. Also, unlike friends or colleagues, I don't typically socialize with clients or know many other people they know. I am a safe person to tell things to that they might not share with other people. A few other personal factors also come into play in my conversations with clients. One, I consider myself an armchair therapist. I enjoy listening to people's problems and though untrained, I offer up pretty sound advice when asked, and sometimes when not asked. Two, I have an intense natural curiosity about the sociology of people and what goes on in their lives. I am fascinated by human perception and behavior. Three, I have almost no filter and, like a three-year-old, I will ask whatever question comes to mind. Four, once a client has begun to reveal startling personal information, I cannot help myself from seeing how much I can pull out of them.

The next time Steven came in, he wanted a back and chest wax which gave him more time to talk.

"How are things going?" I asked him. This and 'have you got any big plans for the weekend' tend to be my pat conversation starters.

"Aahhh, not so great. All this stuff with my wife and me ... I need to figure out what to do."

"Steven, I'm sorry to hear you guys are having issues. I know how difficult that can be. How long have you been married?" I asked.

"God, it seems like forever," he said, rolling his eyes.

"That bad huh?"

"It's been like eighteen years and we met really young. We just don't seem to have anything in common anymore."

"That's a long time. It's not unusual for people to drift apart. I know a handful of couples who kind of lost their connection and were able to reacquaint themselves and find new things in common. It's not easy but it's possible. Do you have any children?"

"We were going to but we never got around to it. It never seemed like the right time for her," he paused for a moment. "Plus she gets on me all the time about my drinking."

Ding, ding, ding. There it is–big issue number one.

"Plus, man I can't *believe* I'm even talking about this" he proclaimed while he reached down to his pants from the wax table, and pulled out his phone, looking at it to make sure he hadn't auto-dialed someone. "We haven't even had sex in like eight years."

Ding. Big issue number two.

"*Wow,*" I said genuinely surprised, "that must be very difficult." Again, women make these kinds of admissions all the time, so my radar is completely off-line.

"Yeah, I'm so used to taking care of myself in the shower, it's fucking *humiliating.*" Okay, now women don't usually share this kind of detail. I have never had a women say, "yeah, he hasn't touched me in years, so, you know, I have to get the Hitachi out. It's so humiliating." And, I think if that happened, a husband's interest would probably be piqued. So yes, now my radar is on, but still, these are people problems and I hear people problems all the time. Steven has a problem and I might be the only person he has to talk to. Uh yeah, except his wife maybe. That would be better, huh?

"Have you and your wife considered going to a therapist?" I offered.

"Yeah, but we owe so much money, and I don't think it would make a difference at this point."

"I think a lot of marriages can be fixed with help. Therapy can help you identify the issues and figure out a plan to move through them. Even if you think the marriage is unfixable, it could also help you navigate making the moves to separate and divorce in a healthier way."

"Yeah and sometimes I think that this is just what marriage becomes after a while."

"I don't think walking around your partner on eggshells and going eight years without sexual intimacy is normal."

"I know, right? I bet *you're* a lot of fun," he said, looking at me like I was a juicy rib eye. Oh god, here we go, I thought.

"My *husband* thinks so." I said, making a point.

"Do you think I need to wax my ass," he asked, abruptly changing the subject.

"It isn't about what I think, it's about what you think."

"Well how hairy is too hairy?"

"Most women expect that a man is going to have some bum hair and you're a fair-skinned guy, not very hairy so chances are, you don't need to wax your bum." At this point, with Steven over sharing, I did not need our waxing to become more intimate.

"Okay, you're probably right."

BACK, SAC & CRACK: THE BAD BOYS OF WAXING

We wrapped up the wax, Steven paid and tipped me and made another appointment for a few weeks later. His mild inappropriateness didn't put him on the No-Fly List because one, he tipped well, and two, his mildly inappropriate comments didn't make me feel intimidated or threatened. Steven was a client that I felt like I could handle. Sadly, in our society, most if not all women get used to and probably accommodate a lot of inappropriate male behavior. I have had veterinarians who won't stop talking at my tits, college professors who asked me to have drinks, dads of babysitting gigs "stop short" on the drive to take me home. When I was an ad rep for a radio station, I had a married, male client of mine "accidentally" grab my ass during a walkthrough of his empty, charity haunted house during off hours. When I left him an email the next day explaining that I needed to resign the account because I was no longer comfortable working with him, he left me a long phone message about how I must have gotten the wrong idea about what happened, and blah, blah blah. No, I'm pretty sure I got the idea that you wanted to fuck me in that empty haunted house and your ass-grab game was designed to feel out how willing I was to work for my supper. Loud and clear, asshat. Yeah, I'm a girl, but counter to nearly every mainstream media message I get, that doesn't make me stupid.

A few weeks later Steven was on my table again for another back and chest wax. I start with his back. We make some small talk and then he goes right into the talk about his problems at home. He tells me how they never have sex, how he has to masturbate in the shower. It's the same stuff he talked about last time and now I am kind of tuned out, half-listening because I've heard it and just figuring he needs to vent. I ask him to turn over so I can

128

wax his stomach. He just keeps talking about "taking care of himself" and looking at me and it's starting to make me really uncomfortable. He tells me about how he likes to get massages and I think this is more my territory, the spa stuff. He tells me that he gets massages just to get someone to touch him and I think about how massage is so beneficial and the how therapeutic it can be. I tell him about when I first moved to Southern California and didn't have any friends and looked forward to my weekly massages for that very reason. I continue waxing his stomach and he unbuttons his pants and pulls the front edge of them down until just about the top of where his public hair begins.

"Can you wax a little further down this time?"

"Sure," I say and as I am pressing the strip he keeps talking.

"I get hand jobs at the massage place once in a while. No big deal. Because, you know, a guy gets good and tired of doing it himself all the time." Strike one.

I just feel weird now because that was just way too much information. I finish waxing his lower stomach and I don't know if it was the pain or just to get my attention, but he kind of grabs my arm and looks at me. Strike two.

I move my arm from him and step back a little. I quickly wipe him off. "We're all done," I tell him.

"I don't know," he says as he pulls down his pants and points his ass in my direction. "Maybe I should wax my butt."

Strike three. Okay, I think I'm done now. I tell him that unfortunately I don't have time for that today as I have another client waiting. My instincts could have been off, but I was pretty sure that the next appointment, Steven was going to ask for a hand job. It's No Fly for this guy.

In spite of the discomfort I have occasionally had to endure with gross behavior, it is also oddly comforting for someone to exceed my limit. It lets me know I still have some.

FOURTEEN

....

NO, I DON'T THINK YOU NEED
TO BLEACH YOUR ASSHOLE

"So Chris, do you work?" asked Stacy, the perfectly polished wife of my husband's new boss, as she handed me a second glass of wine. My husband had just landed the job the week before, but John and Stacy had graciously invited us to their lavish company holiday party just the same.

"Yes, I'm an esthetician, I own a day spa in Long Beach."

"Nice. So you do massage and that kind of thing?" she asked.

"I myself am not licensed to do massage but we do offer massage therapy. I do mostly facials and waxing."

"Oh it's my lucky day," Stacy said excitedly. Then her tone turned grave, "look at these wrinkles around my eyes. You are the professional. Tell me, what should I do?"

"Your skin looks really good," I offered cautiously. This was after all, the boss's wife, the unofficial VP of the Department of Boss Relations.

"Seriously, even my crow's feet have crow's feet and my skin is dry, but now I am getting these pimples on my chin," she said, aggressively poking her finger at a small, nearly imperceptible bump.

"Well," I offered, "hormonal fluctuations can be a cause of adult female acne. Have you had any changes with your cycle or hormones?" I asked, realizing as I said it that I was asking my husband's boss's wife about her period. I guess at least I wasn't live tweeting it.

"Yes, I will go a few months with no period and then bam, I get it for two weeks, and heavy like you wouldn't believe."

"Is it possible that you may be peri-menopausal?" I asked carefully since menopause can be a hot button for some women.

"It's certainly possible, I haven't had my hormones checked but I used to be as regular as can be, and now my period is all over the place." The phrase 'period all over the place' made my brain conjure up a disturbing visual, not unlike the crime scene of a very expressive serial killer. I smiled and tried to refocus.

"My recommendation would be that if your skin is dry and breaking out, you start with a mild salicylic product, like a cleanser. The salicylic acid breaks down dead skin and can help clear up acne. It's my first line of defense with adult acne and most clients respond very well. And the exfoliation is great for fine lines too. I can email you some product suggestions if you like," I offered. In this business, we say fine lines not *wrinkles* or *crow's feet*, underarms not *pits*, upper lip not *moustache*, it just sounds better.

"Oh Chris, that would be so great. You said you did waxing, like brows and stuff?"

"Yes, brows, upper lips, legs, bikinis..." Why, I thought, could I never just answer yes to a question without elaborating?

"*Ohhh*, do you do that *Brazilian* waxing?" she asked, her eyebrows raised.

"I do."

"I have wanted to try that but I have been too scared."

"It's not so bad."

"Chris, I'm not afraid of the pain. Hell, I delivered my youngest at nine pounds five ounces, natural. I'm not afraid of a little hair pull. But I am a little bashful."

"If you've had kids, you should be used to people hanging around your business."

"You'd think so right? But since I had the kids, my body is all tore up and it's never quite recovered. I have stretch marks and things are not so pristine. Jesus, I had hemorrhoids with both pregnancies, and I think as I have gotten older my skin down there is getting darker. Christ, my ass must be a mess, thank god I can't see it. Have you heard of this new thing Chris, this ass bleaching?"

Oh, god, I thought, how did we get *here*? This is so *inappropriate*. I searched the room looking for my husband.

"Level with me Chris," she kept going, "as a professional, do you think I should bleach my asshole?"

Fuck me, fuck me, fuck me, I scanned the room searching for my husband to extricate me from this. I saw him talking to a group of other engineers. He met my glance and gave me a thumbs up like I was doing him a favor chatting up Stacy, completely missing my come-rescue-me-or-we-will-never-be-invited-back-and-you-may-not-have-a-job-on-Monday look. I am already wildly inappropriate on my own without inappropriate leading questions from a person with whom I should have a friendly, yet formal social relationship. I say things that get me into trouble all the time without anyone else's help thank you very much. I have navigated less tricky situations and failed. Most people might just clam up in these situations, but not me. When I get nervous I go into hyperdrive talking mode and sometimes cannot stop myself. Plus, she *asked* me a question, would it not be equally inappropriate to leave her hanging? What can I say that won't be wrong? In my head I am already preparing for the conversation with/apology to my husband later, "you know I can't drink and be expected to talk to people without using bad words or giving them advice on the color of their winker. I thought we established this a long time ago."

As I tried to form words that could not be used against me, I was saved by a smoking, sea food tower. Two waiters walked into the banquet room carrying what looked like a four-foot, tiered tower of crab claws and giant shrimp and all sorts of stuff on crushed ice. Even better, buried somewhere underneath was dry ice making it look like the whole seafood tower was smoking. Everyone in the room rushed to the colossal seafood tower and I was saved from extreme social humiliation and possibly an up-close look at Stacy's purportedly discolored anus. The real lesson of this story? Never underestimate the power of giant shrimp to get you out of tricky social situations.

Stacy wasn't even the first or last person to ask me what I thought about butt bleaching, just the only person at a company dinner party to ask. When people find out I am a professional Brazilian waxer, I get asked all sorts of questions. I think because the job is one part lurid and one part clinical, people are curious. I do see naked people all day long, but I'm not a doctor, but I'm not a porn star either. I understand the curiosity, like the first time I waxed a porn star and I asked about a million questions, because you know that the way it appears or the way you have imagined it cannot be the way it actually is. So there is this impulse to pull the curtain back and have a look for yourself. There have been a few left-field questions, but the questions I get most are about the service itself.

Does it hurt?

No honey, it doesn't hurt at all. Of course it hurts, silly. The first one is the worst because the hairs are mature, thick and essentially glued to the follicle. The pain is sharp but short-lived. Most clients report that their second wax is only a fraction as painful as the first. With routine waxing, the discomfort diminishes greatly.

Why do we have pubic hair anyway?

Have you ever heard the phrase 'if there's grass on the field, time to play ball?' No? Me neither. Evolutionarily speaking, pubic hair signaled sexual maturity and baby-making readiness. Now we have things like a driver's license to give the all clear. It is also thought that hair traps body odors and pheromones that used to be sexually arousing but have been replaced by more alluring modern smells like Axe chocolate body spray and Jessica Simpson's *Fancy* scent.

What exactly makes a Brazilian a Brazilian?

Ask a dozen different waxers this question and you will probably get a dozen different answers. I have always considered a Brazilian to be all hair removed south of the border, the "border" being your clitoris. So no lip hair and no bum hair (to fit the rather tiny, G-string Brazilian bikinis) and then any variation of hair up top: none, manicured natural triangle, petite triangle, landing strip, and postage stamp. If you want to keep some hair and are not sure what your waxer has in mind, I suggest getting very specific with a paper and pencil.

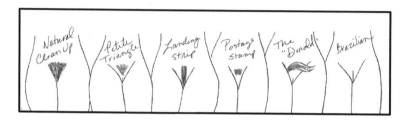

How old do I have to be to get a Brazilian wax?

Funny story, when is it not a good idea to have a handsome, naked guy stretched across your waxing table? When he slips about still being in high school. Some salons have a policy that if you are under eighteen, you need to be accompanied by a parent. Just yuck. I really don't like the idea of sixteen year-old Suzy's mom standing over me while I wax her daughter's chatch. I have definitely waxed minors before but always accidentally. The seventeen year-old teen I waxed was homosexual, very comfortable with himself and going *cruising* on a Mexican cruise with his family. It was definitely not the normal scenario. One time I waxed a client's thirteen year-old daughter's underarms. She was trying to save her daughter the pain of shaving but her daughter hated it and her resistance made me really uncomfortable. I think beauty rituals that cause pain should be saved for adulthood.

Why are the Kardashians famous?

Okay, this has nothing to do with waxing but don't we all ask ourselves this?

Ripped

Do I need to get totally naked to get a Brazilian wax?

Look, I can give you a disposable paper G-string but they are ill-fitting, look silly and I am going to see every part of you regardless of the poufy, paper panty. I usually instruct clients to go naked from the waist down. You–in all your nudeypants splendor–are easier for me and you are going to get a more meticulous wax without the fuss. A lot of my female clients like to come in a dress or skirt that they can just hoist up, remove panties, get in, get ripped, and get out. I love efficient women.

Can I get a Brazilian wax when I am menstruating?

I have seen it all during the span of my waxing career: the sweat, the tears, some poop, and yes, my share of period blood. Listen, I don't have a problem fording your rusty river. Just pop in a cork, tuck in your string and we are good to go. Sure, I have had anxiety dreams where I accidentally pull someone's tampon out and it goes flying across the room, but it's never *actually* happened. My only caveat is that waxing during your period may be more uncomfortable. For one, you have probably been binging on salt and vinegar potato chips or Oreos and may not be feeling super confident getting naked for one of my overpriced whipping sessions. Second, you might be cranky and not likely to tip me as generously as usual. But if you can't easily schedule around it, just come as you are.

Am I still a feminist if I wax my vagina?

This is a tough one. First of all, yes, you can still be a feminist, even if you personally ascribe to the painful beauty rituals our culture currently holds in favor. That being said, I can think of far more empowering ways to embrace your femininity than waxing your lady parts. I am a vehement feminist and I still wax my vadge and wear high heels. I'm a product of my time but still fighting the good fight.

Is my vagina ugly?

Have you read Chapter 9, *Elephant Ears*? Chances are, your vagina is absolutely normal and perfectly pretty. Some women harbor a great deal of insecurity about their lady bits and 99.9% of the time it is totally unnecessary. Yes, there is a wide variation of cha-chas but don't compare yours to the vaselined, pinkified, air-brushed twinkies you see in men's magazines. The "high-brow" porno mags of the day Photoshop the shit out of women's kitties until the women look anatomically more like plastic dolls than flesh-and-bone, breathing women. The best place to see real vaginas, if you need an in-the-flesh comparison, is cheap pornography. But make sure you haven't just had lunch. By the way, speaking to the heterosexual women, men don't care. One of your labia might be slightly longer than the other, or maybe your skin is more brown-toned then petal pink. Men are so happy to be allowed to see you naked that their brains don't register the finer details of your punani. They just see magnificent muff offered up ever so generously from you to them. On the off chance that you are one of the small few who are carrying around generally odd equipment, then sport that nasty thing with confidence. If I have learned anything from the Internet, it is that someone, somewhere, is looking for someone just like you.

Can I bring my boyfriend, mother, best friend, child, therapist, agent or spiritual healer in the room with me during the wax?

Listen honey, I like an audience as much as the next attention-starved only child, but no. Your boyfriend watching me wrist deep in your vagina is a little too close to a threesome for my comfort. Even if our twenty minutes together just ends up in his spank bank, which trust me, it will, it smacks of smut. If you need your mom to come in and hold your hand while I rip hair out of your vag, then you are just not ready for a wax. Now best friend is a gray area. This is the only exception I have occasionally made. Your best friend is going to make you giggle, which is good because it distracts you from the discomfort. But it can be bad too–if you move while you giggle, you are going to get all sticky and I will have to spend an extra ten minutes cleaning you up. Time is money baby.

Can I get a Brazilian if I have vagina jewelry?

I love the client but I hate the vagina jewelry. Seriously, the clit ring and labia chains are the devil. I get why people do it. Well, kind of. I'm guessing that they ran out of fingers and ears and just like jewelry a lot. It's really on the same page as waxing and vajazzling and any other secret, sexy beautification. Still, for a waxer, that stuff just gets in the way. One of my favorite regulars has a clit ring and for years she has come in monthly for her wax and never once did I get it on her jewelry until recently. There is nothing more awesome then trying to use your fingernail to scrape wax off of your client's clit ring. Thankfully she and I already had great rapport and laughed through it. But I'll be honest, I took a Xanax afterward.

Can I have sex right after a Brazilian wax?

If you want your cha-cha to look like a pimple-faced teenager the next day, go right ahead. I understand that your boyfriends and husbands will probably want to inspect it right away. (And I am not dismissing you lesbians; you just usually have more self control). So let him have a look but hands off the merchandise and no sweaty coupling until day two. When the hair is pulled from the follicle, it leaves a small invisible hole and the perfect pathway for bacteria to enter the skin. I'm not saying your man is a cootie carrier, but he is. The bacteria, naturally present on his skin, may be different than your own and when you mush your parts together, you transfer sweat and bacteria and, frankly, who knows what else. These bacteria can work their way into the follicle and cause fun little pimples all over. Then you will want to pop these pimples and someone will walk in on you giving your muff a facial and it may make its way onto YouTube and you will either become a star or forever shunned—there is no way to predict these things.

Will I get aroused during the wax?

I did have a client who said the mix of gentle powdering, oiling, and the warm wax application was *confusing* her vagina but then the hair pulling started and her vagina was more angry than confused. If you are a woman, getting aroused is unlikely. If you are a man, there is about a fifty-fifty chance you are going to get a boner. It's okay, really it is. Take a deep breath, make a joke if you want, and I'll work around it. Just don't masturbate in my room after I exit or I will cut a bitch.

Will you make me get on all fours?

I guess the question is, do you want to? Because I can accommodate most requests. Kidding aside, when I started waxing, this was the position most waxers put people in to wax the bum area. The problem with this position is twofold. First, it is not a position that affords one a great deal of dignity and many people get very self-conscious about it. It's called doggy-style and not *Queen-Victoria-Meryl-Streep-style* for a reason. Second, most people, if asked to get on all fours, would give me a little demure bend-over and I can't get at anything anyway. In order to wax the ass, I ask people to pull their legs in toward their chest and this opens up, if you will, the perianal area so that I can remove all of the winker fuzz. I still see every bit and bob, but it's more like yoga and less like your porn debut.

How often can I get a wax?

Everything in moderation right? Well probably not things like meth, crack, and apparently Jessica Simpson. In the hands of us humans, most things can be abused and waxing is no exception. Most clients come in every four to six weeks or so. You can always do an in-between touch up for a big date or pool party but come in more often and you risk falling into waxorexic territory.

I had one Brazilian and I hated it, how do I know if it was something the technician did or if this service is just not for me?

For any of you who have had the Brazilian, if your esthetician does not use hard wax you are being shafted (pun intended). Hard wax is a stripless wax that is used in the following way: a light coating of oil is smoothed over the skin; the wax is applied and as it cools; it shrink wraps the hair so that when you pull it (no paper needed because it becomes plastic-like), it removes the hair but keeps the skin from getting irritated. When it comes to waxing the testicles or the labia, this wax is essential or you can very easily end up with raspberries and torn or lifted skin. This type of wax also greatly reduces the amount of discomfort you experience and generally your skin recovers more quickly. So, if your technician was not properly trained and/or used soft wax only and you had an unpleasant experience, it is very likely that you could have a much more positive outcome with a better waxer. It still hurts. That part doesn't change.

Is it ever weird doing what you do?

Are we talking about the waxing or the other weird things I do? Yes, once in a while, things get kind of weird, but without those times, this book just wouldn't be. I get asked this all the time. Is it uncomfortable being up to my elbows in crotch? Does it ever get routine looking at all that vagina? Is it weird to have a front-row seat to buttholes day in and day out? It's true, I have come home on more than one occasion after a day spent waxing upwards of fifteen women and tell my husband that I am so tired of looking at vaginas. Still, we all get bored at our jobs now and then. Waxing a vagina is no different for me than waxing an underarm, or a leg, or an upper lip. And it's probably no different for me than it is for a podiatrist to see yet another foot or a tax accountant getting tired of looking at receipts. I'm very matter-of-fact about it because I've done it thousands of times. Still, working as a Brazilian bikini waxer, things are only going to get *so* routine. Part of the fun of my job is just when I think I have finally seen everything, something new pops up, figuratively and sometimes literally, like when a guy gets an erection.

Can I do a Brazilian at home by myself?

You can. I've done it. But I did it after having two done and paying close attention to what they were doing. Also, I'm pretty awesome when it comes to learning things quickly and you probably are not. If you are brave, there are tutorials online that can help, but be forewarned: this is how I get a lot of my new clients. They try, get mid-way through a botched job and call me to fix it. Unless you are very good with your hands, bendy, flexible, adventurous, and have already birthed an actual human and thus are intimately acquainted with real pain, better to just find a pro and let her do a good job for you.

Why do so many guys like it totally bare. Is that pervy?

Just because your guy wants you hairless doesn't mean it's because he wants you to look like a child. Guys like it bare for a number of reasons. For one, men are visual creatures and born hunters. Pubic hair naturally camouflages their favorite bits.

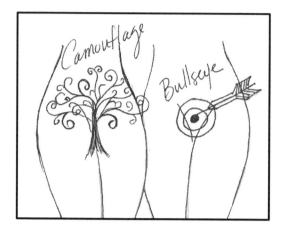

When your business is waxed clean, they get an unobstructed view of their target. For some men, the idea that you have gone through a painful ritual to beautify your business is arousing. It's like you are serving them your goodies on a silver platter. It's captivating and tempting in the way that only a smooth, bare vagina can be, or for that matter, a smoking seafood platter.

Should I bleach my asshole?

No I don't think you should bleach your asshole. Do you know how many times I have been asked that question? Too many times. Come on, this is like teeth whitening for your bung and you know how there are some people who whiten their teeth so much they turn a weird sort of neon, bluish white? Some things are better left natural. I have never seen an approved color palette for ass but most of the ones I have seen look the same. Most anal bleaching is done with repeated applications of a cream containing hydroquinone. Now, never mind that hydroquinone is banned in most of Europe and is a known carcinogen, does anyone really have the time to apply cream twice daily for several weeks in order to get a pinker pucker and brighter bung? If you really have the time for this level of maintenance, then I suggest you drop the bum bleach and devote that time to something more altruistic like being a Big Brother/Big Sister or something. On second thought, drop that idea because I don't think the Big Brothers/Big Sisters organizations want a bunch of ass-bleachers around impressionable children.

FIFTEEN

························

SHITLISTER OR A-LISTER: TREATING YOUR WAXER RIGHT

*I*n college I majored in political science with the intent of going to law school. I was a very good student and had my choice of law schools. Then I let my own insecurities convince me that the competition would be tougher with all of these talented students brought together, and that maybe getting straight As at my state college wasn't going to prepare me for the academic rigors of law school. Sometimes I wish someone would have told me to just go, try it, face my fear, and if I failed, well, it builds character or at least humorous, self-defense mechanisms. Instead I got a sales job in radio. I moved around and moved up, finally working for a consulting company that worked with the radio and television industries. I spent eight years doing something that I was good at but for me, was mostly a real soul suck. Then at the tender age of twenty-eight, I chucked it all and surprised everyone by going to beauty school. I paid around seven-hundred dollars at the time for my reeducation and in just a few months, I was a part of the pink-collar workforce.

The pink collar refers to the bevy of mostly female service jobs. Working in the service industry is all about working with people, so of course, the job is a mixed bag. There are clients that become friends and there are people who give you money to do a service and are pleasant but don't care to get to know you. There are great clients and difficult clients, and lastly, there are people you would rather pull out your own nails than work on.

I have given a great deal of myself in the service of my customers. I have given my time, my shoes, a separated shoulder, countless backaches, sciatica, sore feet, ruined clothes, missed movies. I have skipped hundreds of meals to fit in last-minute clients, I have eaten a sandwich in one-bite servings every half an hour on an overbooked day. I have quietly gummed thousands of Altoids so as not to offend tender clients with coffee breath. I have stroked egos, thankfully *only* egos. I have reassured women about their bodies, their jobs, their kids, their marriages. I have held their hands while they sobbed over some lost love or lost parent in an exposed, vulnerable moment in my room. I have offered up my trials and tribulations for their amusement and distraction.

Every job I have ever had or ever heard of has involved occasionally dealing with difficult people. What makes a person difficult, of course, depends in part on what job you are being asked to do. As the consumer of a product or service, sometimes you care about the person you are buying from and sometimes you do not. The already surly lady at the DMV? I don't think there is much I can say to make her nicer to me, though that never stops me from trying. The woman who waxes your vagina is a good person to be nice to. There are a number of ways a waxer can make it hurt less or hurt more. Think carefully before you cross that imaginary pink line and become one of the customers we bitch about when you are not in earshot.

So what kind of customers make the shit list? Girls who want a full Brazilian but are afraid to take off their panties. That's like asking a dentist to clean your teeth with your mouth closed. Coming in sick to appointments will also get you shit-listed. I'm touching you, often your face and you are touching things in my treatment room. Please, if you know you are sick, just wait rather than be a modern Typhoid Mary. Once when I was pregnant, a client told me at the end of a back wax that he had just recovered from chicken pox. He had potentially exposed me to chicken pox, which, had I not already had as a child, could have caused birth defects or a miscarriage. If I am sick, I cannot work. If I cannot work, I don't get paid.

Also nearing the top of the shit list are people who don't show up, cancel last minute or are chronically late for their appointments. Also, people who arrive 40 minutes late for a half-hour service and then get angry with you when you can't take them. I am nearly always on time and I know most of my clients appreciate knowing when they will get in and out and can plan their day accordingly. Late clients make me run late and that makes me look bad. Sure, it happens once in awhile but if you are always late, expect to get bumped or have to wait as you may have gotten bumped for a client who arrived ahead of you. And if you *are* late, you can adjust your tip upward to show contrition. Do that and your esthetician or stylist will leave an extra fifteen minutes to accommodate you next time.

I also loathe people who treat me like I am dumb. These are usually the people who have a very set idea about the women who work as estheticians and stylists. Of course if they treat me like I am dumb but leave a good tip because they feel sorry for me, then they are fine. People who do not tip are probably the worst, except for people who imply that they want a hand job—that's *probably* worse than not getting tipped.

I also have an aversion to people who are not diligent wipers. Yes, it happens, but really just wipe your butt better, people, okay? I hate people who steal stuff out of my room. Just because I leave you alone to get dressed doesn't mean it's a free for all. I have had many a thing go missing from a cheap but pretty ring to large, professional-size products to my reading glasses. Seriously people, stop stealing.

When someone lands on my shit list, they may still get an appointment, but all bets are off. The naughty-list people are ones I will move at the drop of a hat. If you are a shit lister and an A-lister wants to come in where you are currently scheduled, guess what happens? You get moved. If you want to be treated like a VIP you have to earn your way into that club and it's not always about money. Do you know how many pro bono cha-cha waxes I've given to clients going through a rough financial time? Lots, because I take care of the people that took care of me.

Do you want to become an A-Lister? Do you want special treatment, a kind ear, a last minute appointment, free samples, and a gift at your wedding? Want to be a person we love? Want us to honestly tell you which stylist in our salon is great and which one just started using drugs again? In the beauty industry, probably the whole service industry, we love people who tip. We also really appreciate customers who tip and who bring us something from Starbucks. We *cherish* customers who tip, bring us something from Starbucks, *and* actually know what we drink. We love and remember clients who give us presents at Christmas. Don't think it goes unnoticed, it doesn't. Not everyone gives their waxer or stylist a holiday gift, so if you do, even a small one, it really makes an impression.

We appreciate people who apologize when they are late or miss an appointment. We love people who apologize when they are late or miss an appointment *and* adjust their tip upward as an act of contrition *and* bring us Starbucks *and* presents. Those are the best people of all. We appreciate the people who tell their friends about us because referrals translate into food on the table. We remember the people who call or write us after the fact and tell us when we have been especially good or accommodating. We love people who pay cash. And of course, we like people who treat us like people.

SIXTEEN

··

HAPPY ENDINGS

A s much as I favor smooth concrete over a grassy yard, when it comes to my own personal landscaping, I had never seriously considered permanent laser hair removal. Why? I'm not sure. Maybe it was just in case. It could be that I wanted to hang on to a full and versatile pubic wardrobe. A woman likes to have options right? I guess I thought that should a lush seventies bush make a comeback, I could end up desperately searching for a natural and affordable merkin on Ebay. Speaking of lush seventies bushes, have you see Demi Moore's 1980's Oui magazine spread? If ever there were a poster child for hair removal, it might just be Demi. That was neither demi nor semi but some serious full coverage. The phrase referenced most with regard to those pictures is *hair diaper*. Not even a modest, full-coverage swimsuit could hide that kind of fur. If you haven't seen them, consider yourself spared. Step away from Google and don't judge, everyone had big hair in the eighties. While I would never aspire to the full coverage hair diaper, I did consider that I might want some hair on my vagina at some point. If my face is going to age and wrinkle over time, what else will show its years? When I was still single, I worried that my mate for life might end up being some handsome hippie that would have to begrudgingly come to accept my fully shorn kitty should I not be able to coax a natural bush from my years of deforestation. Or maybe feminism would take a dramatic leap forward and the subsequent backlash would target us women who had permanently removed all of our pubic hair. While I rarely sported more than a week or two's regrowth, I wanted to hang onto the options should my tastes or situation change. What does all of this say about me? It certainly illustrates the breadth and depth of my anxiety, that there is *nothing* I cannot spend time worrying about, including the future state of pubic hair trends.

As much as I hated making permanent decisions about anything, after years of waxing, I had to face the fact that I would not always be able to wax my own vag. I had always waxed myself save for a few times when it was simply more convenient to have a coworker do it, like when I was eight months pregnant and couldn't see my vagina anymore. As I approached the end of my thirties, I was no longer the human pretzel I once was. Bending over naked while seated in a chair with my leg above my head was still possible but not *nearly* as flattering at thirty-nine as it was at twenty-nine. Lately, after waxing I have felt physically defeated and self-conscious. Seeing all my perceived flaws in such unforgiving light made me feel seriously dumpy--exactly the opposite of the wax's intended effect. And waxing my ass had devolved to require even more complicated maneuvering and the addition of a hand mirror.

I was also no longer waxing professionally and getting out the big wax pot every 6-8 weeks and waxing my vag at the very same desk I wrote at was proving messy. I come by writer's block and procrastination naturally enough without needing excuses like

Ripped

sticky elbows and pubic hair on my desk to throw me off track. After years of free Brazilians done by me or at the able hands of a trusted coworker, the idea of making an appointment, getting there early and paying fifty to seventy dollars for the privilege was just not in my realm of possibilities. Getting waxed for free for so long set the value, it simply was not a service I was willing to pay full boat for. Likewise, as someone who was known for my meticulous work, I am not exactly the easiest to please. I've had only one other esthetician in all my years leave me as smooth and pretty as I left others.

Certainly as a staunch feminist, the idea of letting it go wild occurred to me. I mean, I already had a man, a good-looking one at that. Plus, we were married with kids, busy with careers and life. He certainly wouldn't let some pubes get in the way of enjoying our marital bounty. Still, even if I burned my bra and "watered my garden", the ground was pretty over-farmed. I had tried once or twice to grow a bush for varying reasons, kind of like a man growing a moustache or beard just to see if he could. After years of waxing, it just doesn't come in the way it used to. I have so little hair that it always ending up looking like the lawn in an empty, forgotten lot or a man trying to coax cheap hair plugs into a lush mane. Even if I wanted my pubic hair to be my crowning glory, it was never going to happen.

I was happily married to a man who liked me the way I liked myself, fully weed whacked and smooth as stone. I had worn the hair on my head roughly the same color and same way for the last 15 years, I was fairly resistant to change. Even if my husband died in a tragic accident and I was forced to find comfort with Liam Neeson, chances are my preference for hairlessness would remain

153

unswayed. Another consideration was that I was not getting any younger and if I waited too long to make a decision about permanent removal, I could end up with all my hair gone except a batch of greys, as laser does not at this point work on grey hair. So with all of that in mind, I decided to put my vag under the expert care of the Princess Leia of laser cha-cha waxing and zap that hair off for good.

It was a little weird going in because I am used to being the technician or certainly as well versed as the technician and in this case, I was not. I had a basic understanding of how it all worked but beyond that nothing. Would she put me on all fours? I wondered. Would my tender labia burst into flames when lasered as my friend predicted? Would I be able to have sex that same day, my husband pleaded. No, stop asking already.

I already knew of a great laser clinic that probably wouldn't set my vagina on fire, so I didn't have to do much homework. I called and asked all of my questions. I asked about pain and was offered a topical numbing cream but the laser was already pretty pricey so I decided to opt out of the extra forty-dollar labia lidocaine. I scheduled an appointment and waited. Like any savvy woman, I used my pussy laser appointment to garner all kinds of favors from my husband. Any time we had a standoff over who was going to drive one of the kids somewhere or whose turn it was to make dinner, I would look at him pleading "but I'm getting my pussy *lasered* for you." It was possibly the best excuse ever because he was happy I was doing it and would *never* consider doing the same for me. It was a watertight, get-out-of-jail-free card, basically a vacation from my life. Kids need help with math? Sorry, I'm getting my pussy lasered in a few days, I really have to take it easy.

Unload the dishwasher? Sorry, saving my strength for the pussy laser. Sell some cookie dough and giftwrap for school? With the pussy laser and everything, I'm pretty sure I'm supposed to just lay here and play on my phone. Never mind it was as much for me as it was for him, the impending pussy laser got me a solid week off.

On the day of my laser hair-removal appointment, nerves set in. I had shaved the night before as they suggested and now my skin, used to waxing, was on fire. Angry red streaks marked where I had scratched like a dog with fleas. "Stop scratching," admonished my husband.

"I can't, it's so *itchy*, I hate shaving." Between the itching and the anticipation of pain, I was a wreck.

"You don't have to do this, you can cancel you know, I don't care."

"Don't tell me you don't care when I'm about to unleash a Tomahawk missile strike against my cha."

"Well, I *care*, but you know what I mean. I'm ok if you decide this isn't something you feel like doing."

"I made the appointment. I don't want to wax anymore or god forbid shave," I said scratching again. "I'll just take a Xanax and lean in."

"Knuckle down? You sure?"

"Yep, and I want you to know that it's probably going to take a week for that shit to recover. I'm pretty sure bed rest is recommended."

I drove to my laser appointment with plenty of time to spare because I am a girl who likes to be on time. Roadwork thwarted my punctuality and I languished in stand-still traffic thinking I would be late for my pussy laser. I was only a few minutes late and the receptionist quickly got me checked in.

"I'm sorry I was late, there was construction," I apologized.

"No worries. Everyone seemed to hit the same delay. Sarah is running a few minutes behind, did you want to get the numbing cream?"

"No. I've waxed my whole adult life," I said dismissively. "I think I'll be fine."

There were three nurses performing laser hair removal and as I watched two women emerge from their treatments looking stricken, I became more anxious. I went through the procedure in my mind trying to alleviate my fear of the unknown, but it only made it worse. I think at one point in the visualization, my vagina actually *flinched* and I rethought the numbing cream. I sidled up to the reception desk, "I think I'd like to try that cream after all."

She gave it to me with the same look nurses probably give mothers-to-be when they finally opt for the epidural after haughty, steadfast proclamations of doing it the "natural" way, which on a side note, seems odd to me, considering no one asks a man getting a vasectomy or a person having a hernia repaired to if they want to go "natural". Coincidently, I gave birth the way my grandmother did, fifties style knocked all the way out after three epidurals failed to work and I needed an emergency C-section. I just woke up and boom, had a baby! If general anesthesia or horse tranquilizers were offered for laser or waxing, I bet more men would have it done.

I took my numbing cream in hand and headed to the bathroom realizing that the entire waiting area had heard the conversation and was now aware I was going straight into the bathroom to frost myself like a birthday cake. I locked the door behind me and scooped two finger fulls of vag balm out and rubbed it all over my cha not forgetting to generously numb up my butt too. I washed my hands, put the top back on the cream and returned to the waiting area. The lady I sat next to looked at me with her eyes raised. Yes, I *washed* my hands, I wanted to tell her.

In spite of my deep breathing, visualization, and affirmations, I was still very anxious. I am prone to anxiety and have had more than my fair share of panic attacks. I'm pretty sure there is nothing worse then being in a room of strangers completely convinced you are about to die or throw up on yourself. The mix of the actual fear of death, fear of embarrassment, and fear of the fear of death and embarrassment themselves are enough to make me feel like I am going to keel over like one of those goats that just go stiff and fall over. When a panic attack is coming on, my fingers start to tingle, so you can imagine my dread when it started happening right there in the waiting room. Oh god, I am going to have a full blown panic attack before my pussy laser. I started obsessively checking in with my body when I realized that only the fingers on my right hand were weirdly tingly–the same hand I had used to slather my business with numbing cream. I realized it was the cream, but by then I was so worried that the worrying itself would bring on a panic attack that I actually started to have one.

Fuck me and my reptilian brain, I thought. I took several deep breaths and reasoned with my frantic mind that there was no dinosaur, this was just my limbic system run amok. It was a simple pussy laser–nothing to be afraid of. Okay, well nothing that was going to *kill* me. I got my anxiety under control to a tolerable nauseating din. I looked at the room and it seemed like every single person in there was looking at me. With anxiety, it can be hard to figure out what is real and what is your mind on overload. Was everyone looking at me because I had been muttering out loud about fainting goats and pussy lasers or was it just my paranoia?

I didn't get to delve into that bit of crazy because one of the treatment doors opened and Sarah the nurse and her patient came out. The woman wore a skirt and her legs were almost pulsing red. She handed the receptionist her credit card politely and I wondered why these freshly tortured women didn't react more appropriately considering the circumstances. Had even just *one* woman ever come out of the treatment room crying, slap the nurse, and then throw a bunch of bills at the receptionist before issuing a primal scream and running like a lunatic from the clinic? What have we women been reduced to when we pay hundreds, even thousands of dollars for the chance to get tortured to comply with increasingly complicated beauty rituals and then politely smile like our genitals *aren't* on fire and *thank* the person who did it? Seriously, we women need to unionize or something.

It was my turn and I followed Sarah back into the treatment room. The lobby was air conditioned and chilly so I had put on a heavy sweater I brought with me. Sarah asked me to take my pants and underwear off and the treatment table was covered with a nice, soft, thick pile blanket, like one you'd see draped over a couch. I stood there naked from the waist down with a sweater and shoes still on looking super sexy, I'm sure, and waited for her to tell me what to do. I didn't believe she wanted me bare assed on her good blanket. She looked at me like what are you waiting for and I looked at the nice blanket nervously.

"Oh," she said, "yes, let me put the sheet down," and with that, she put a disposable sheet over the fluffy blanket. I couldn't stop thinking that the nice blanket was totally out of place at a hair-removal clinic, kind of like shag carpet at a whore house, ick.

Sarah took a squeeze bottle and squirted a whole bunch of what looked like lube all over me. "Chilly," I said smiling at her like a crazy person. She took a wooden tongue depressor and evenly spread the gel. The laser itself wasn't too bad. Amazingly when the pain started, and it began to hurt, the anxiety about the pain went away. Brains are so stupid.

"It's not hurting at all," I said smiling at her like I was just the most serene woman ever with an impressive pain threshold.

"Not at all? Are you feeling anything?" she asked.

"It's warm," I said, "a little prickly maybe." I thought it was much more comfortable than waxing. She moved the hand piece and looked at my skin.

"Hmm, it should hurt more, I think I need to turn it up."

Sure, I mean, I did want it to work so if turning it up meant a better result, I was all for it. She started pulsing again and I think the machine was actually turned on this time because it really hurt. It hurt so much I had a hard time staying still and I can do a complete Brazilian wax on myself without so much as a wince. I had read that laser hair removal felt like someone snapping rubber bands on your skin. Who does that anyway? It seems like a very bully-friendly reference point. It didn't feel like rubber bands and it didn't feel like pin pricks. It felt more like being horsewhipped with a hot curling iron.

And, in addition to the pain, the whole thing was very gooey. There was a lot of gel as she slid the laser over my muff and in between my butt and I couldn't help but feel like I had made a mess on her nice table.

"That's it," she said as she cleaned off the laser and reholstered it to the giant machine it was tethered to.

She stood there waiting for me. I wanted to grab the thin paper disposable sheet and wipe all the goo off my cha and in between my bum but with her standing there waiting, it felt unseemly. So I just pulled my things on over my gooey cooter. As I walked up to the checkout area, I felt like what I imagine it feels like when you have completely shit yourself. With every step I took I swear to god I heard sounds like when you pull a rubber boot out of the mud.

I went home and headed straight for the bathroom to change my pants. My husband followed me in, no doubt curious as to how the pussy laser went. He watched as I inspected the gel all over my jeans.

"That good huh?" asked my husband.

"Shut up, that's gross. This is some sort of gel for the laser to glide over," I told him.

"Uh huh, sure it is."

I have been back a few times and laser is good, but it never gets everything. I still wax every few months when I just can't stand the seven hairs. I started a waxer and a waxer I will stay.

SEVENTEEN

....

PUSSY PLAYLIST

usic can be a powerful mood setter. When I went into
the delivery room to have my youngest daughter, I was
armed with the best preggo mix cd ever. I had Lovely
Day by Bill Withers for a soothing, soulful happy calm, Comfortably Numb by Pink Floyd in hopes of musical pain relief. I had
Salt-N-Pepa's Push It for a little hard labor motivation and Guns
'N Rose's Sweet Child of Mine to welcome her in. Little did I
know that my labor would take four days and end in an emergency
C-section. I got a screw in my baby's head, a probe in my vagina
to measure contractions, three epidurals, more than my share of
Pitocin, some Ketamine horse tranquilizer (street name Special K)
and some superglue holding me together where they had sliced me
open like an overripe watermelon, but I never did get a chance to
listen to my special mix cd.

But I was not deterred from coming up with a Pussy Playlist
that I hope you'll find fitting for your next waxing. So if the mood
strikes you, queue up the Pussy Playlist for your wax session, as a
gift for your favorite esthetician, as background music for clients

with a sense of humor or as just a little motivation to get you through your defuzzing.

Torn and Frayed- The Rolling Stones
Rip Her to Shreds-Blondie
Scream & Shout - will.i.am featuring Britney Spears
Lip Service-Elvis Costello
I Could Hurt You Now- Aimee Mann
Shake It Off- Taylor Swift
Tears Dry on Their Own- Amy Winehouse
Supermassive Black Hole- Radiohead
Cruel Summer- Bananarama
This Summer's Gonna Hurt Like a Motherfucker – Maroon 5
Just Lose It–Eminem
Girl On Fire–Alicia Keys
Started From the Bottom–Drake
All the Young Dudes–David Bowie
Lips Are Movin'–Meghan Trainor
Worth It–Fifth Harmony
Do That To Me One More Time–Captain & Tennille
Twist and Shout–The Beatles
I Say a Little Prayer–Dionne Warwick
Lay Down Sally–Eric Clapton-
Brown Eyes–Lady Gaga
Big Girls Don't Cry–Fergie
Half the Man I Used to Be–Stone Temple Pilots
Break My Body–Pixies
I Cry–Flo Rida
Black Hole Sun- Soundgarden

Ripped

Can't Be Tamed–Miley Cyrus
Blank Space–Taylor Swift
Pink Moon–Nick Drake
Bizarre Love Triangle–New Order
Take It Off–Ke$ha
Both Sides Now–Joni Mitchell

A KNOWLEDGMENTS

....

Years ago I sat in a dark theater listening to David Sedaris do a reading. My husband and I spent nearly the entire sixty minutes laughing so hard we could barely breath. I was eight months pregnant at the time and I actually peed my pants a little. I had long been a fan and knew David was funny, but somehow seeing this quirky guy with his own way of viewing the world light up a room full of people made me see that *everyone* has their stories. When a part of me wanted to write something very serious and important, watching David gave me the courage to put fingers to keys and tell some of my own stories, inviting readers to peek into how I see the world. So thank you David for giving me a kind of 'tipping point' moment.

Thank you to all of the clients, including Kelly, Melissa, Julie, Michael & Mary, Vicki, Tina and far too many to name and friends, like Ion and Terrie who laughed at my stories as I recounted them. I hope you weren't laughing out of politeness because, uh, I wrote this book.

Thank you to the large tribe of women I worked alongside including Jennifer, Simonetta, Kathleen, Larissa and Nicole. Thank you to the assistants that kept me on track including Kaitlyn, Jolieke and Jacqueline.

Thank you to Patte McDowell for encouraging me to "just get in the pool" and be brave anytime I got tangled up in feelings that my stories might not matter or be good enough.

Thank you to my formerlyfun.com blog readers and group of writers I became acquainted with through it. To have a community of writers talking about writing and writing about writing was invaluable and really, quite fun.

Thank you to my editor Tiffany Hardy who is a gifted writer herself but also a kind and thoughtful editor. Not only did her edits make this book better, her corrections made me a better writer. And her notes about the parts that made her laugh were often the gas powering my engine. Thank you to Claire Konishi for helping me translate what was in my head to IRL for my cover design.

I need to thank my husband Gene Duquette for his love, belief in me and everything from trying to make my doodles work to solving my tech problems to bringing me diet cokes with extra lemon, foot rubs and encouragement and of course letting me put things about him in the book without ever even once telling me I shouldn't use our pillow talk or things that make him look kind of goofy. Don't worry honey, I know how *you* like to be thanked. And of course, thank you to my three amazing children: Josh, Clare and Izzy who add to the weird that is my life in the very best ways.

Last, I want to thank all of my clients, even the stinky weird ones, *especially* the stinky weird ones because you gave me some pretty awesome material, material that I have told and retold over the course of many years making other *nicer* clients laugh while they toughed out a wax.

ABOUT THE AUTHOR

Christine Duquette lives in Southern California with her husband Gene and their three children. These days she writes professionally and can be found at stellarwebwriting.com or blogging and answering beauty and other questions at thebarespa.com.

28943102R00098

Made in the USA
Middletown, DE
01 February 2016